BECOMING SISTER WIVES

BECOMING SISTER WIVES

THE STORY OF AN UNCONVENTIONAL MARRIAGE

KODY, MERI, JANELLE, CHRISTINE, AND ROBYN BROWN

Gallery Books

New York   London   Toronto   Sydney   New Delhi

Gallery Books
A Division of Simon & Schuster, Inc.
1230 Avenue of the Americas
New York, NY 10020

First Gallery Books hardcover edition May 2012

GALLERY BOOKS and colophon are registered trademarks of Simon & Schuster, Inc.

For information about special discounts for bulk purchases,
please contact Simon & Schuster Special Sales at 1-866-506-1949
or business@simonandschuster.com

The Simon & Schuster Speakers Bureau can bring authors to your live event.
For more information or to book an event contact the Simon & Schuster
Speakers Bureau at 1-866-248-3049 or visit our website at www.simonspeakers.com.

Photo Credits
Cover photo by Allison Easley
Group photo on first page of insert courtesy of Liz Bowles Photography
Wedding photo of Robyn and Kody on third page of insert courtesy of
    Bryant Livingston Photography
All other insert photos courtesy of Kody Brown Family Entertainment, LLC

Designed by Davina Mock-Maniscalco

Manufactured in the United States of America

10 9 8 7 6 5 4 3 2

Library of Congress Cataloging-in-Publication Data is on file.

ISBN 978–1–4516–6121–7
ISBN 978–1–4516–6122–4 (ebook)

To all those who lived and loved before us, in secrecy,
unable to acknowledge their love, marriages, and life publically,
we dedicate our story to you.

BROWN

Kody m. Meri
(1990)

Kody m. Janelle
(1993)

Mariah, *daughter, b. 1995*

Logan, *son, b. 1994;*
Madison, *daughter, b. 1995;*
Hunter, *son, b. 1997;*
Garrison, *son, b. 1998;*
Gabriel, *son, b. 2001;*
Savanah, *daughter, b. 2004*

FAMILY TREE

Kody m. Christine
(1994)

Kody m. Robyn
(2010)

Aspyn, *daughter, b. 1995;*
Mykelti, *daughter, b. 1996;*
Paedon, *son, b. 1998;*
Gwendlyn, *daughter, b. 2001;*
Ysabel, *daughter, b. 2003;*
Truely, *daughter, b. 2010*

Solomon, *son, b. 2011*

Dayton, *son, b. 2000;*
Aurora, *daughter, b. 2002;*
Breanna, *daughter, b. 2004*

CONTENTS

BECOMING SISTER WIVES

PROLOGUE

Kody

I am sitting in a room off of the grand ballroom in the Beverly Hills Hilton. I almost can't believe I'm here. I'm a small-town boy, not some Hollywood superstar. This glittering place is a far cry from my current hometown of Lehi, Utah. The occasion is the Television Critics Association biannual press tour at which networks announce their fall lineup of television shows to the media.

Onstage they are playing a clip from a new show on the Discovery Channel. It's about Greenpeace crusaders who are devoted to saving whales. It's a hippie version of that channel's smash hit *Deadliest Catch*. This is the kind of show the critics are expecting—the kind of show guaranteed to draw attention without polarizing the audience.

My show is a lot more controversial. It's the first of its kind. Like the Greenpeace activists onstage, I, too, am taking a stand. But I have no idea how my fight will play out in the court of public opinion. I have no idea how critics, the audience, and the American public are going to react to me. I'm getting nervous.

I'm sitting in a chair getting my hair and makeup done. Makeup! I grew up on a ranch in rural Wyoming. I never, ever thought I'd wear makeup, let alone have a team of people apply it, making sure I'm camera ready. The stylist asks me casually, "So what's your show about?"

"Oh," I say, trying to be as offhand as possible, "it's about my family. I'm a polygamist and I have four wives."

The stylist stops fussing with me for a second. I can see the shock in her eyes. I know what's she's thinking. I'm an average-looking dude who looks more like a surfer than a religious fanatic. How could *I* be a polygamist?

After I'm done with hair and makeup, I'm ushered backstage with my wives. We wait anxiously as the 120-second teaser for our show plays on the big screen in the auditorium. They've added some pumping music to the trailer, trying to infuse my family's life with tension and intrigue.

My heart begins to pound. I'm breathing shallowly. What have I done? I'm about to expose my family to the world. I'm about to do the very thing most polygamous families live in fear of—I'm about to go public.

I know that I'm putting my family at risk. My wives and I could lose our jobs. Our children could be tormented at school. But I'm tired of hiding. I'm tired of living like a second-class citizen. I'm tired of lying about my life. I have a wonderful family—a perfectly happy family—with beautiful wives and beautiful children. I don't want us to live the rest of our days in fear. I am about to ask America to accept us.

I grasp my wives' hands in an informal prayer circle. We draw strength from one another, and from our faith in God. We renew our commitment to our beliefs. I steady myself. The world is ready, I think, to hear our story. The world is ready to accept us for who we are and not shun us for our beliefs. I drop my wives' hands as we are called to the stage.

• • •

Let me introduce you to the real face of polygamy.

When people hear the phrase "Mormon fundamentalist," they probably think about a small subset of our population—the Fundamentalist Church of Jesus Christ of Latter-day Saints. For too long this organization, and the handful of abusive men who ran it, have been the poster children of polygamy in America. Until recently, the FLDS was run by Warren Jeffs, who has been found guilty of child sexual assault and is now serving a life sentence in prison. He ruled his organization with an iron fist, creating a climate rampant with abuse and fear. He not only tolerated but also promoted child brides. He summarily reassigned the wives of men he deemed unworthy to new husbands. These are not my beliefs. This is not my world.

While we share a belief in the principle of celestial plural marriage, I want to make it clear that the practices of the FLDS have no place in my universe. We belong to a different religious community, one that has several thousand members worldwide. In our faith, incest and spousal abuse are serious crimes, which, when discovered, result in immediate legal action.

I'm sure when most people think of Mormon fundamentalists they think of long, modest dresses and old-fashioned hairstyles—something you might see in an old Western movie. This only covers a fraction of polygamists. If we weren't on TV, you wouldn't be able to pick my family out of a crowd. We dress like anyone else—maybe a tiny bit more modestly, but definitely modernly. Our kids go to public school. They watch TV, go to the movies, play computer games, go to parties, and listen to popular music. They play sports, wear makeup (sometimes too much for my liking), and participate in school activities. Basically, my family is not all that different from yours.

Our sect is one of the more liberal branches of Mormon fundamentalism. Unlike some other fundamentalist Mormons, we accept the Church of Jesus Christ of Latter-day Saints as a legitimate faith. We follow the same scripture they do. In most beliefs and practices, we differ very little from the LDS church. Of course, the one area in which we do diverge is in our belief in "The Doctrine of Celestial Plural Marriage," which we call "the principle." Although not every member of our faith enters into a plural marriage, we still believe that it is a crucial step in our personal spiritual development.

Celestial plural marriage isn't something we take lightly or take for granted. It's a calling, something we are summoned to by God. It's a commandment in our scripture, fundamental to our belief system. Its intention and design is specific to our personal development and spiritual growth. Not all people in our sect enter into polygamy despite their belief in the doctrine. Some never find the right partners with whom to live the principle. However, when the opportunity for plural marriage is placed before us, and when we are called to it—it seems wise to accept.

Religion is by nature elitist. Everyone wants to believe that his way is the right way. Too many people, regardless of their faith, are small-minded enough to imagine that their beliefs, their doctrines, and their rituals are the only way to be saved or to know God. I'm not self-centered enough to entertain these thoughts. In no way do I imagine that my family members are the only people who got it right.

God speaks to each of us in His own way. He calls a person in that person's language and reaches individuals in terms they will understand. What I'm called to do is not what you are called to do. I don't consider followers of another religion any less worthy in God's eyes or in mine. I don't believe that what's appropriate for one person is necessarily appropriate for all. The principle is my calling. It's probably not yours—and that's fine with me.

The principle of plural marriage is sacred to me and to all fundamentalist Mormons. It's not something I've come to casually or flippantly. It's not easy and it's not something I recommend to anyone who is not prepared for the challenges.

Building a complex family from four separate marriages has its challenges. My wives and I have had to learn to be understanding, kind, compassionate, and patient. We have had to develop ourselves morally and ethically.

The demands on a plural family are far greater than those on a monogamous couple. Since we have to consider the sensitivity of other wives and other marriages on an everyday basis, plural marriage consistently challenges us. It makes us confront our shortcomings and overcome them. We have to learn to handle our jealousy, contain our aggression. We have to check our selfishness. There is no room for ego in plural marriage.

Although we know these things, we are by no means perfect. Each member of my family has his or her flaws. Every day, we must work toward a higher level of communication with one another. In the end, our acceptance of the doctrine of plural marriage allows us to transcend our limitations and become enlightened. It challenges us to be the best version of ourselves in this lifetime.

I know people probably misinterpret what I do. They probably think I'm wife hoarding—that I'm satisfying my carnality at the expense of my wives' feelings. I know there are people out there who assume I'm some kind of macho pig. While this couldn't be further from the truth, I understand that this misconception comes from the perceived imbalance in the practice. Why can I have multiple wives, yet my wives cannot have multiple husbands?

In the first place, that is not our commandment. Second, when my wives are asked if they would take a second husband, they emphatically answer, "Not interested." Perhaps there are people out there for whom taking plural husbands is a viable lifestyle. Perhaps there is a religion where this is a sacred way of life. But this is not our faith.

Each of my wives has come into our family of her own free will. Choosing to join a plural family has been their choices, their preferences. It's something they prayed over, then sought out of their own volitions. Believe it or not, some of them made the first move, asking to join my family even before I proposed.

When I say I love each of my wives wholly, passionately, and eternally, I am telling the truth. I believe that with each of my wives I share a destiny and that together we five adults were predetermined to be one family. We believe on a very deep level that we belong together in an absolute fashion. We are meant to be.

So how can I love four women? It's a fair question and an easy one to answer. Loving them is simple. It's like breathing, waking up in the morning, putting one foot in front of the other. It's one of those things you do unconsciously, something so deeply ingrained into your psyche and your way of being that you never question it.

It's hard to explain *how* I love my wives to someone who is not inside the principle. The simplest analogy is of a mother who is pregnant with her second child and worries that she will not love this one as much as she loved her first. It's an honest fear. But on the day her new baby is born, she loves it as much as her firstborn. She loves it independently of her firstborn. She loves both of her children because they are her children, but she loves them individually for their different qualities. She loves one because he's a remarkable athlete but she doesn't love him any less because he's a terrible student, even as she loves the other for her sense of humor and her scholarly habits.

It's the same with my wives, but on a much more intimate level. I love them for different reasons—for their different strengths and their different passions and talents. I love them for their weaknesses and their humanity. But I don't love one more or less than the others.

Being in love with four women is easy, but not easy at the same time. Since my wives are so different from one another and so independent, each of my marriages is distinct and each is dynamic in its own way. I can't always pinpoint the moment I fell in love with each of my individual wives, and I don't always feel that love all the time, but the love is so deep I can't imagine being without it. Our bond is the kind of thing you know you need for the rest of your life, not in a codependent way, but in a way that bonds us so deeply that when I have been away from any one wife too long, I feel an emotional ache.

To be honest, I am not sure if any one of my wives could fulfill all my needs, nor do I believe that I am fulfilling all of theirs. Janelle and I can talk business. With Christine I can enjoy the lightness of being together. With Meri the world is structured and organized, her house is peaceful and in order. When Robyn came into the family, she brought about an emotional honesty that required me to start dealing with things I'd avoided.

A lot of people wonder if there's a plan or a system for taking a new wife. If there is, I've yet to see it. The only requirement is that I have a spiritual connection with a woman I'm considering courting, and that she feel connected not only to me but also to my family. In some cases in our faith, the woman makes the first move. If she feels drawn to a certain family or man, she can make her interest known through her father. But she must be willing to join herself not only to her potential husband but also to his wives.

Of course, a man must have the permission of his wives to consider a courtship. After all, the woman he wishes to court is going to be as much a part of his wives' lives as she will be of his. If my wives didn't want me to pursue a relationship with someone, I'd have no choice but to obey their wishes. My first duty is to them.

I married my first wives relatively quickly and relatively young by conventional standards, if not those of our faith. Each relationship developed along its own lines, for its own reasons, with its own trajectory. After sixteen years together as a family, I found myself in the position to pursue a new courtship. I was as surprised by this as my wives were, and I knew that it would involve a serious adjustment on their part. If I hadn't had their blessing, I'd never have gone forward with courting Robyn. Family always comes first.

Standing backstage in Los Angeles, I'm growing nervous. I know that when I go public there will be questions about sex. It's America's obsession, after all. Even though my show is a family television program on a family-oriented network, the world wants to know what goes on behind closed doors. All I'm going to say is my marriages aren't different from anyone else's in that respect. As in most relationships, passion is always there, but it waxes and wanes. With each wife, we go through phases. There are the demands of work and kids—all the regular things that interfere with a couple's private life. The one constant is that I keep my four marriages distinct and discreet. There is no overlap, no "sharing," nothing untoward or salacious.

There are many benefits and blessings to our lifestyle. We are a large family, and not one of us will ever know loneliness again.

We are a team, a strong foundation on which we've raised our children. My wives support one another. They can lean on one another for small favors and for large ones.

Our biggest struggles have been financial. There have been lean times. It took me longer than I'd hoped to establish myself in a career, especially with wives to support. Of course, all of my income goes to the family. I try my best to allocate money evenly and according to who needs it most. If a wife needs a bigger car because she is expecting a new child, I prioritize that. If another wife needs help completing a major home repair, this takes precedence over something more trivial.

All of my wives contribute significantly to both their individual households and the family as a whole. Before we went public, several of them worked full-time. They support their kids, and what is left over they kick into large group expenses such as mortgages. If one of my wives chooses not to work in order to stay home and look after our kids, I make sure she is taken care of. If another wife makes a bundle while her sister wife is looking after the kids, she will share her bounty. If someone has a windfall from tax returns or inheritance, then she usually shares a good portion of it. Although my wives are fiercely independent and entirely self-sufficient, they never let anyone go without. We are a family of equals.

I want to stress that equality and fairness are our guiding principles. Since there is only one of me and four of them, I am often considered the patriarch. Unfortunately, this word has acquired a negative connotation these days. I'm appealed to on a regular basis, simply because I'm the common denominator—I'm the basic element that my wives and children share. I'm a father to all the children and a husband to all my wives. Despite this, I rarely make unilateral decisions. If asked, I will choose the direction in which the train runs, but my wives are the ones who keep it on the track and running. They are the force behind our family.

I know the world wants definitions to understand us. They want to know who is the smart wife, who is the homemaker, who is the silly one, who is the mean one. But I won't let my family be pigeonholed. Our relationships are complex and they are constantly evolving. Ours is a process that elevates us and allows us to abide in God's presence.

I have a goal in mind of what my family is supposed to be and look like. It's supposed to be happy and peaceful and free. I imagine a unity that comes from joy, not from overwhelming sacrifice or pain, anguish, and suffering. I don't want my family to suffer for the sake of God, because if we are suffering for the sake of God in this life, we may not be happy with Him in the next one.

Privately we've arrived at this unity, this peace, but publicly we are still subject to prejudice. We are misunderstood. We are outsiders. And this is what has brought me here to Beverly Hills. This is why we are about to show our faces to the world and announce that we are polygamous and we are proud!

I never want my children to live in fear. I never want them to be forced to deny any part of themselves. I want them to live openly as siblings. I don't know whether my children will enter into the principle. I don't know whether they will live the life of polygamy. Some will be called to it and others won't. But regardless of their choices, I want the world to be a more free and understanding place for them to grow up in. I want them to feel safe in their family, and if they choose polygamy for their future, I want them to do so knowing that they will not be treated as second-class citizens. What we do with our bodies and our hearts is the most important choice of all.

My heart is pounding as I step onto the stage. I can feel the smile plastered on my face. It's my defense mechanism—this silly grin. There's a sea of faces in the auditorium. The audience is silent. I can't tell what they're thinking. I feel the smile slip from my face. My heart is in my mouth.

Suddenly the audience begins to clap. I feel the atmosphere begin to warm. I sense that they are drawn to us. I think they are ready to hear our story.

PART ONE

MATRIMONY

Chapter One

MERI AND KODY

Meri

I spent the early years of my life living in California with my parents, both of whom were devout followers of the Church of Jesus Christ of Latter-day Saints. When I was a baby, my mom had a friend who left the LDS church because she practiced plural marriage. When my mom learned about this, it piqued her interest, and she began studying the principle as well. Soon after, she suggested to my dad that the family move to Utah. He didn't know her religious reasons at the time, but he said sure, let's move—though it took them four and a half more years of research and studying the principle before they actually did. We finally moved to Utah when I was five years old.

It was my mother who urged my father to take his first plural wife. He did, and she joined the family when I was only five, but I still have fond memories of her. Unfortunately, it was a short marriage with no children, and she left two years later. When I was ten, my mom and dad once again brought a new wife into the family. I didn't think there was anything strange about it—in fact, I was excited. I was a shy kid and didn't make friends easily. When I found out that the woman my father was courting was from a large polygamous family, I was thrilled to have the chance to get to know a whole new group of people and be able to make more friends. Our family grew quickly. Eventually, my father took four wives in addition to my mother. In total, I have twenty-seven siblings!

I was in a slightly easier position than many of my siblings who came from my father's second, third, fourth, or fifth marriages. Since I was the child of my father's first marriage, his "legal" one, it was simple and natural for my father to be my father in public. Since polygamy isn't widely accepted, for the other kids, it could be more difficult to acknowledge their father publicly. To my father's credit, he "owned," that is, acted as a true father to, every one of my brothers and sisters.

Growing up, I always assumed I would live the polygamous lifestyle. It was the tradition in which I was raised. My biological parents and my mother's sister wives all seemed happy for the most part. Of course there were the normal ups and downs that happen in any family. I loved being part of a large family; it felt normal and comfortable. My parents, however, never pushed me toward the principle. They wanted me to make my own decisions and come to plural marriage, if I chose, through my own route.

My parents' only rule about religion was that I had to go to church, but this isn't so different from millions of parents around the world. It was always made clear to me that whatever religion I embraced as an adult—whether our branch of fundamentalism, LDS, or something else—was entirely up to me.

Despite the fact that I was shy, I managed to make a number of friends outside our church group. I worked at a portrait studio and became friendly with many of my coworkers, which helped me to overcome my shyness. Perhaps because I interacted with so many people outside my faith when I was a teenager, for a time I really questioned whether or not I was going to live the principle of plural marriage. I was struggling to find my way and discover my own identity within our close-knit community and the requirements of our faith—and then I met Kody.

Kody

I was raised in the LDS faith. Both of my parents were devout Mormons. However, when I was fourteen years old, my mother pulled me aside and explained to me some of the doctrines of Mormonism that are a little more intense. One of these is that of celestial plural marriage. The moment my mother described the principle to me, I had a feeling that this was something I was going to follow. I had no idea how or when, I just knew.

Of course, being young and stubborn, I battled hard against this calling. In the LDS church there's absolutely no opportunity to explore plural marriage. It's simply not done. Plural marriage is one of the few things that sets the Mormon fundamentalist faith apart from followers of the LDS church. The religions are similar, but this one difference is astronomical. Embracing it meant leaving the faith of my childhood forever.

When I was nineteen, I was sent on my LDS mission to southern Texas. During the two years I spent proselytizing for the Mormon church, the doctrine of plural marriage was constantly on my mind. It spoke to me. It called to me. But I still had no idea what to do with this summons.

While I was away in the ministry in Texas, I got a letter from my mother telling me that my parents had been excommunicated from the LDS church and had joined a fundamentalist Mormon faith. I thought, *Well, this is interesting.* But I was still too hard-headed to see it as a sign that I should follow in their footsteps. My parents' excommunication from the Mormon church broke my heart. I was deeply concerned about their spiritual welfare, but God spoke peace to me. I continued my service in the mission field and finished my two-year calling.

By the time I returned from my mission, my father had taken a second wife. My mother had written me dozens of letters about how wonderful her sister wife was, so although I had never met my new mom, I was ready to accept her completely. She deserved my respect and my love, simply because my father had married her.

When I returned to Utah from Texas, I immediately experienced the remarkable warmth of the principle of plural marriage as my mother had explained it to me years before. The warmth and love I imagined would go hand in hand with a polygamous lifestyle were no longer an unattainable ideal. They were real and concrete and precisely as I had imagined they would be. My mother was away, but here was another woman who loved my father and whom my father loved, and by extension, we grew to love each other as mother and son. It was an easy and wonderful evolution.

Even though my parents had converted to fundamentalism and I'd discovered for myself the warmth of the polygamous lifestyle, I was still uncertain about converting myself. I began associating with members of my parents' new church and attending their gatherings. I thought I knew what I wanted, but it took me a while to make a commitment. Then I met a girl named Meri, and that changed everything.

Meri

I first noticed Kody at church. Our church group is quite close-knit and has been together a long time, so any new face really stands out. He caught my eye, and I believe I caught his. Some-

one introduced us, but beyond a brief hello, I don't think we said a word to each other. I was eighteen, and I'd never been courted by a guy before. Shoot, I was so quiet that I'd probably never even been *noticed* by a guy before! So nothing of a romantic nature crossed my mind during that first meeting.

That summer I attended a camp for girls of our faith. One of my fellow campers, a girl named Christy, was here from out of state and had a photo of her brother who was attending our church in Utah. When she showed it to me, I immediately recognized Kody.

A few months after camp ended, Christy came back to Utah from her home in Wyoming to attend a wedding. She invited me over to the house where she was staying. I walked in the door and there was Kody, sitting on the couch! He said, "Hi, Meri! You're the Meri my sister is always talking about."

I was shocked that he knew my name. I was used to my friends getting all the guys while I went pretty much unnoticed. It was good to be seen for once and not to be overlooked for my shyness. I was a little taken with Kody right off the bat. He was definitely cute, and had a great attitude. He was talkative and engaged me in conversation, and made me feel comfortable around him. Neither courting nor dating were on my mind at that point. He was the brother of a good friend, and that was how we began our friendship.

The next day Kody and Christy came to meet me as I got off my shift at my job at a portrait studio in the mall. The three of us went to lunch and then to an evening get-together. I felt comfortable around them, as if I'd fallen into a new and safe friendship.

Over the next few days, I began discovering what a fun guy Kody was. He was always laughing and smiling. He had a good attitude and a positive outlook on life. He really was outgoing and positive. I was impressed with the strength of his convictions and the depth of his spirituality. After knowing him for just a few days, I found myself liking to be around him and spending time with him, and wondering what direction this new relationship would take. One night, while his sister was still in town, we went to the home of some friends of his family for a party. There were quite a few people there, but every once in a while I would catch Kody looking at me. When our eyes met, he'd give me a little smile. It made my heart race. Unfortunately, a few days later, Christy returned to Wyoming. Since she was the reason I'd been hanging out with Kody in the first place, I didn't really think that he and I would see each other as much as we had been.

Thankfully, I was wrong. The next week, Kody and I continued running into each other at church events. Eventually he asked my dad if it would be okay if the two of us went out to grab a bite to eat. I know it seems pretty old-fashioned that a young man would need my father's permission to go out with me, but our faith has specific morals to uphold and protocols to follow. Therefore, out of respect for me and my dad, Kody wanted to request my father's permission for our association. Anyway, there was something flattering about a young man going to the trouble of getting my father's approval before taking me out.

My father was an excellent judge of character and warmed to Kody immediately. My dad had a good handle on people. He had no problem with Kody and me "hanging out," which soon became the description we jokingly used for our relationship. He knew me well enough to know that we would be appropriate with each other, and knew he had nothing to worry about in my new relationship. Now that we had my father's approval, Kody and I could get to know each other in earnest.

Maybe it was because of me or maybe it was purely because of his growing interest in our faith (I like to think it was a combination of the two), but Kody started spending more and more time associating with people from our church. I usually found myself somewhere nearby. Kody was, and always has been, a loud and enthusiastic presence. It is hard to miss him in a crowd. Back then, I was quickly learning that Kody is the guy everybody wants to know and be around.

At first when people noticed us hanging out together they would ask Kody if I was his sister. I had been a member of this church since I was five years old, but I was so quiet and shy that many people had simply not noticed me. Now that I was spending time with Kody, people began to take notice.

Before Kody arrived in our group, I had been a wallflower. Now I began coming out of my shell. It was nice, but it was strange. I was experiencing the people and places that had been most familiar to me in a whole new light. I was participating instead of standing on the sidelines. I was spending more and more time with him and starting to hope that our relationship would go beyond friendship.

But then, Kody broke my heart.

After we had known each other for a few weeks, when I could no longer deny that I was falling for him, Kody came over to my house. We were sitting on the couch, waiting for my mom to get home. Kody really enjoyed my mom's company and wanted to spend some time with her, which pleased me and gave me hope that things were becoming more serious between us. This hope was short-lived.

At the precise moment I'd expected him to make some sort of declaration to me, or at least hint at his feelings toward me, he said, "I can't get involved in any relationships with girls right now. I like our friendship, let's continue that."

I was devastated. But I fought not to let it show.

Kody

I'm a hopeless romantic and too easily infatuated. When I was growing up, I suffered all sorts of little heartbreaks. I had a careless dating style. I would dive into a relationship before considering my true feelings. Often I'd find myself holding a girl's hand, then I'd look over at her and think: *Why am I holding her hand? I don't really like her.*

During my two years in the ministry in Texas, I promised myself that I would never again kiss a woman until I knew for sure that I was in love. When I returned home from my mission and began seriously considering converting from the LDS church to Mormon fundamentalism, my mother told me that I should take time away from girls, or at least from dating them. She knew that I needed to become less careless and discover what it was I truly wanted from a relationship and whom I truly loved. My mother sat me down and said, "The next time you find yourself infatuated with someone, why don't you just try and be friends? Don't rush into a romantic relationship right off the bat. Be friends and let something develop."

That decided it. I told myself I was done with dating carelessly. I was done chasing girls. I urged myself to be patient and to learn how to be friends with the next girl I became interested in. Meri was my experiment in friends!

Meri was so cute and sweet when I met her that I had a hard time suppressing my hopelessly romantic nature. She had a remarkable purity about her. I had a sneaking suspicion that we were soul mates, but because of the promise I had made to myself, I rejected this notion. I was determined to be Meri's friend until I knew her better and could confirm my suspicion that our destinies were intertwined. I was glad that Meri and I kept finding ourselves spending more and more time together.

I was excited to be associating with members of Meri's faith. They had an intensity about religion that I found inspiring. Perhaps because their religion was somewhat countercultural and at odds with certain conventional doctrines, they took no aspect of their belief for granted. They examined their convictions carefully and enthusiastically. The members of this group were fully committed to their ideologies and discussed them at length, both debating and confirming the tenets of their religion. Every day I spent with this group seemed to turn into an impromptu revival with profound discussions of spirituality and religion that I'd been missing in the LDS church. Even though I loved my new group of friends and their congregation, I hadn't yet determined whether I should join the faith.

Nevertheless, I kept surrounding myself with people from my parents' new church. A few weeks after I told Meri that I wasn't open to dating, I invited her up to my parents' ranch in Wyoming for Thanksgiving. Meri and I were never far from each other's side during that trip. Naturally, people began to ask if we were dating. It was pretty clear that we liked each other a whole lot more than just "friends." I often caught Meri making eyes at me. I didn't have to ask her how she felt about me—it was written all over her face. I couldn't stop winking back at her from time to time. It was no longer possible for me to deny that I had strong feelings for Meri. She was sweet and innocent, and a wonderful listener. She validated my existence. We became inseparable.

At the same time, I thought this wasn't fair to Meri or me. I didn't want to lead her on, but I didn't want to make a mistake either.

Thanksgiving weekend ended. I had planned to stay with my parents for a few days, so Meri drove back to Utah with some of our friends. This was the first time in weeks that we had been separated for so long. I thought about her constantly while we were apart.

The house was finally quiet, which is remarkable in my large family. All the guests had returned home, and my younger siblings were in bed. I was sitting at my mom's kitchen table, eating ice cream with a fork. The kitchen was dark, but light from the living room spilled onto the floor. Again I thought it wasn't fair to either of us to pretend we were just friends. We were obviously much more than that. I didn't want to drag this out and hurt Meri or myself in the process.

I needed God to answer two questions: Should I join the church I was investigating, and should Meri and I get married? After all, I couldn't marry her without converting, but I wanted to convert because of a spiritual conviction, not because of my love for Meri. I finished my bowl of ice cream and I decided to fast and pray until I knew with deep conviction what path I should follow.

I went to the bunkhouse on my parents' property, which is where I slept. I got into bed and began my fast. After two days of fasting, I decided to drive back down to Utah. Meri's parents had invited me to stay in a guest room at their home. I hadn't eaten since Meri left Wyoming, and I was shocked by how great I felt. I was strong and energetic, as if I were being sustained by a greater power throughout my fast. I felt as if this remarkable strength that persisted without food or water was part of my answer.

When I got to the guest bedroom, I was overcome with an overwhelming feeling of peace, greater than anything I'd experienced before. That feeling, that unbelievable sense of tranquillity and calm, was exactly what I'd been searching for. I had made my decision and I was at peace with it. That very day, I told Meri's dad that I had decided to join his faith. He made the arrangements quickly. The next weekend I was baptized, and I committed myself to the principle of celestial plural marriage and to God the Almighty. Somehow, in the middle of all of this,

I remembered to ask Meri's father for his permission to court his daughter. I guess my conversion really cast me in a favorable light, because he granted it immediately.

After the baptism, Meri and I went to Temple Square outside the LDS temple in Salt Lake City to meet up with friends. I had my answer about both my faith and about Meri. I knew that I wanted to marry her, and I just had a feeling that she would say yes if I asked. But as usual, I was moving too quickly and following my romantic impulses. We hadn't even started courting, but I was already kneeling at the altar.

That night in Temple Square I was wearing an old trench coat from my mission. I turned to Meri and said, "Your hands look cold." Then I took one of them in mine and I put our hands into the pocket of my coat. I didn't want to attract anyone's notice, but I wanted to hold her hand. I had finally become comfortable with our romance, because now I knew this was the woman I was going to marry.

Meri

Even though Kody had told me that he didn't want to date anyone, I still hoped that he would change his mind. When he finally approached my father about wanting to court me, I was thrilled. Kody and I had a wonderful courtship. The fact that we had spent so much time as friends, and knew each other so well, allowed us to develop a sweet, romantic relationship based upon friendship and mutual respect.

Kody and I decided to spend Christmas with his family at their ranch in Wyoming. It had been three years since he had spent Christmas there and I was looking forward to getting to know his family a little better. We had been courting for a month, but we had been hanging out for longer than that. It was impossible for us to hide the depth of our feelings for each other. Everyone knew we were in love.

At dinner, a few days before Christmas Eve, his family kept nagging us about our relationship. They all wanted to know, "When are you guys getting married?" They asked me over and over again.

Finally I shot back with, "Well, he hasn't even asked me yet," more to tease Kody than anything else—and maybe to light a little fire under him.

That night after dinner, when we were sitting in the bunkhouse, Kody asked in a nervous—but cute!—way, "I'm thinking maybe we ought to get married, you know, if you want to."

It was an awkward moment, not at all the romantic proposal girls dream of. Although I did want to marry him, I was hoping for a real proposal—and there was something else holding me back.

I wanted to take some time for introspection, to know from God if this was the right choice for me. During this time that I was taking to check my feelings and validate them with God, Kody and I went ring shopping. We found a ring we both really liked, but we kept looking just to be sure. Kody knew this was the ring for us, though, so while I thought we were still shopping, he secretly had his sister buy it for him.

On Christmas Eve, Kody officially asked me to marry him. He was really nervous. He sounded shy and embarrassed and not at all like his usual self when he asked me to marry him this time. He handed me the jewelry box without opening it or taking the ring out, almost as if he was delivering a package. I thought it was sweet how nervous and unpracticed he was.

"You're supposed to take the ring out and present it to me, not just hand me the box," I told him. But I was just giving him a hard time. I was thrilled that Kody had asked me to be his wife.

I was completely in love with him. I knew he was my soul mate, and that we were destined for each other. We had a strong foundation of friendship to build on. I was so excited to finally be engaged to him, and looking forward to becoming his wife.

In true Kody Brown fashion, he had once again jumped way ahead of himself. He'd asked me to marry him before he'd received consent from my father. The next day, Kody called my dad. The two of them had developed a deep friendship based on faith, spirituality, and understanding, so my dad gave us permission at once.

Kody

I loved Meri. I was certain of it. But I was worried. In every one of my past infatuations, I had been able to explore the possibility of a chemical connection through a kiss. I hadn't done this with Meri, however, simply because it was not appropriate by the standards of my new faith—and because I was waiting for the appropriate time. When we started our courtship, I promised myself I wouldn't kiss her until we were engaged. This strict abstinence made our relationship and our commitment to each other more powerful and meaningful. This was no simple infatuation. It was love that had been established without the complications of physicality, which makes it spiritual above all else.

During the first week of our engagement, between Christmas and New Year's, we met with the head of our church to get his approval so that we could get married. He gladly granted us his permission.

On New Year's Eve there was a dance for the members of our church community. Meri looked fabulous in the peach dress she wore, which accentuated her curves in a way that I had avoided noticing before our engagement. I didn't need any proof that I was attracted to her at this point. I knew it without a doubt and I was very excited about my decision to marry her. It seemed throughout the dance that we were the only people there. The voices and chatter of our friends and family seemed to be just a background hum as we got lost in each other. She was the most beautiful girl in the whole room; I couldn't take my eyes off her the whole night. When I took Meri home and we were saying good night, I leaned in and kissed her. I hadn't planned to do it, but I didn't try to hold myself back. It was a sweet kiss that felt natural and right. It was the best start to the New Year I could have envisioned. That kiss told me that I had made the right decision to ask for Meri's hand. Our chemistry was undeniable.

Meri and I set a wedding date for April 21, which gave us nearly four more months of courtship, and provided the time for us to even further deepen our relationship. This was an important and special time. After three subsequent marriages, I now understand what a luxury this courtship was. Since we had a monogamous engagement, there were no complications from the emotions and feelings of another wife. Meri and I were able to date as much and as freely as we wished. We were able to get to know each other unencumbered and unhindered.

Those four months were wonderful. Our friendship developed into a remarkable love affair. We shared everything with one another. We got to know each other on an intimate yet chaste level.

After that first kiss, we shared many more sweet kisses. It was clear to me that when Meri and I were finally married, there would be no awkwardness between us. Meri was my fiancée and we were very much in love. Our relationship was a typical love story, the kind you see in movies and on TV. She would smile from across a room and I would wink back at her. We must have aggravated our friends and families with how much in love we were. While we were outwardly infatuated with each other, deep down we were becoming the soul mates I suspected we would be from the moment we met.

During our courtship, we were completely carefree. We had minimum-wage jobs that we weren't committed to. We didn't have much money and were trying to prepare for our wedding and honeymoon, but it didn't bother us. We didn't know where we were going to live after the honeymoon. We didn't know what we were going to do, but it was exciting. We had each other, and that was all that mattered.

Meri

Kody and I were married on April 21, 1990. We had a very special private wedding ceremony and a traditional wedding reception. I wore a simple and elegant white dress that I had made by hand, and I had my heart set on Kody wearing a white tuxedo. I look back now at pictures from our wedding and laugh, but with the eighties having just ended, it was definitely the style of the day.

Kody and I chose to spend our wedding night at our new home. It felt special to us to be able to begin our intimate lives together in our own home, rather than in some hotel room. We were deeply and passionately in love with each other. There was no awkwardness between us, everything felt just as it should be. We had plans to leave on our honeymoon the next day, but unfortunately I got sick and that delayed our plans. Although being in this new relationship with Kody was absolutely amazing and wonderful, and we had a lot of fun together planning our wedding, I think my getting sick was just a result of the stress and pressure that comes along with planning a wedding. So for the next three days, we stayed at home. Kody started calling our home our honeymoon cottage. Finally, toward the end of the third day, I felt good enough to travel. There we were, four days after we were married, finally leaving on our honeymoon. We only got as far as Pocatello, Idaho, that night.

Our honeymoon was a typical Kody Brown–style trip—everything was spontaneous and unplanned. We were just so excited to be married and to be traveling with only each other for company. The next day, we made it to Jackson Hole, Wyoming, our official honeymoon destination. We spent a memorable few days there, sightseeing around the quaint little tourist town and exploring our new relationship. We had a magical and romantic experience together, a wonderful beginning to our new life.

After our honeymoon was over, Kody and I settled down in a town called American Fork, about half an hour south of Salt Lake City. Our new life together was sweet and romantic. We spent as much time together as possible, just basking in the love shared between us. I was nineteen and Kody was twenty-two. We didn't have any set plans for the future yet. We didn't have school or careers tying us down. We just wanted our love affair to continue.

During that first year of marriage, we weren't always the most responsible young adults. At one point, we both held jobs that didn't really interest us. We needed to make a trip out of town to see his family in Wyoming, so we quit our jobs and decided to just get ones that we actually liked when we returned home. We loved spending time together more than anything, and before we had kids or other wives in the picture, we were able to live carefree. Maybe we were purely enjoying ourselves, or maybe we were taking our time figuring out what we wanted. I think it was healthy not to have rushed into anything, pretending that we were more mature and knowledgeable than we were.

One thing Kody and I both knew, and had committed to each

other from the moment we got married, was that there would be other wives. Even in the early days of our marriage, we talked about a second wife. We knew it was going to happen, but we didn't know when or how. We would often have discussions about where we would meet our next wife, who she would be, and how we would bring her into the family. On occasion, when Kody and I would meet a woman, he and I would discuss whether she would be a good fit for our family. We knew it would happen eventually, but in the meantime, we were enjoying the time we had together, learning, sharing, and falling more in love each day.

Chapter Two
JANELLE AND KODY

Janelle

I grew up in Bountiful, Utah, and was raised in the LDS faith. My mother had met some Mormon missionaries while in college, and after she graduated, having converted to Mormonism, she moved to Utah to be with others of her faith. My father died when I was two years old and my mother remarried, but my stepfather was not a hands-on father. He was distant and emotionally unavailable. Eventually my mother divorced him. I knew when I got married and had children of my own that I would look for a man who would be intimately engaged in every aspect of our children's lives.

One of the things instilled in you if you grow up LDS is that you are living the only true faith—nothing else will get you to eternal exaltation. Toward the end of high school, I met a student named Adam, with whom I was quite taken. I knew he wasn't Mormon, which meant we had no hope of being together—unless he converted. I called my grandmother and told her about the boy I had a crush on. She recognized his name and remembered that his family had at one time lived next door to her.

"They're in the clan," my grandmother told me.

Many of my relatives are still down south, and to southerners there is only one clan—the Ku Klux Klan.

I was shocked, and told my grandmother so.

My reaction made her laugh. "They're not in *that* clan," my grandmother explained. "They're polygamists."

Until my grandmother told me this, I had no idea polygamists actually existed, let alone lived among us. I had grown up in the LDS church of Utah, but I was unaware that there was such a thing as polygamy. I thought it was a myth or something from the early days of Mormonism, an old-fashioned tradition that had long since been abandoned.

Adam was not completely committed to his fundamentalist faith and I was happy to welcome him to the LDS church. Not long after he converted, we began courting. Soon we were married in the temple, but my husband wasn't really interested in either his new faith or the branch of fundamentalism he'd been raised in. In fact, he had very little spiritual conviction.

His family, however, fascinated me. I would tell my friends, "My in-laws are polygamous." I was proud to know people in a subculture. They were a novelty.

One of the reasons I was so transfixed by Adam's relatives was that they were so outwardly normal. In fact, they were completely conventional and contemporary. They didn't live behind closed doors or practice any strange customs. They worked, they participated in the community, they sent their kids to local schools. My in-laws didn't dress strangely, as some fundamentalist sects did. The women were strong and independent and had an equal say in family affairs with their husbands.

If only I'd been as enamored with my husband as I was with his family. Unfortunately, Adam and I had problems right from the start. We weren't spiritually, emotionally, or romantically compatible. We lived together for only six months before he moved out.

Although my husband and I had separated, I remained close to his family, including Adam's sister Meri. (Little did I know how close we'd eventually become!) At first, I have to admit it was the novelty that drew me to them. But then I began to feel emotionally invested in them. I enjoyed their large gatherings and the complex and generous notion of family that they presented. At the time, Adam's father had four wives and too many children to count—some were adults like my husband and some were still in elementary school.

Adam's parents went out of their way to include me in their events and to make me feel welcome in their lives. Their group was close-knit and inviting. Even though I was still a member of the LDS church, I was always welcome to attend their religious gatherings.

One evening they invited me to a fireside presentation, which is an informal spiritual get-together. My ex-husband's sister Meri was there. Since I had married her brother, I was friendly with Meri. I knew that she was dating a young man, Kody Brown, with whom she was clearly smitten. Although Meri talked about Kody a great deal, I had never met him.

That evening, when Kody walked into the house to join the party, the strangest feeling washed over me. I felt as if I had forgotten something and suddenly remembered it. It was a feeling of relief and recognition. But I was in the middle of a horrible divorce and I had no idea how to handle the sensation Kody's entrance conjured in me. So I packed it away and made a mental note to deal with it later.

My divorce was not yet finalized, so I still attended certain functions with my estranged husband. One of these was Meri and Kody's wedding. If you look at their wedding pictures, you will see me and my ex-husband in several of the photos.

Kody and Meri made a wonderful couple. They were so young and so much in love. They were like teenagers—silly and goofy.

At their wedding, I never imagined that one day I'd join their family. In fact, I hadn't yet considered converting to their faith.

A little more than a year after my own wedding, my divorce was finalized. My husband lost touch with me and spent very little time with his family. But I grew closer to my former in-laws. I entered their family by marriage and stayed when the marriage was over.

Kody

Even when Meri and I were newlyweds, entering the principle of plural marriage was always at the back of our minds. I had a sense in my heart that this was something I needed to do when I was young. I had seen older men marrying women who had children by their first husbands. I didn't think that I should or could bring other people's children into my life and merge my family with someone else's. At the time, I felt that this would be disruptive to the children and uncomfortable for the ex-husband.

After Meri and I were married, Janelle was often on the periphery of our lives. We both knew that Janelle had endured a rough period during her short-lived marriage, and we wanted to make sure that she remained close with Meri's family despite the divorce. We, as well as Meri's parents, were looking out for Janelle purely because we cared about her. There was never any thought in my mind, or in Meri's, of Janelle becoming a wife.

Meri and I often invited Janelle out for pizza or a movie. The women had developed a friendship of their own, independent of Meri's brother. And through Meri, I got to know Janelle. Our friendship was entirely platonic, but I recognized Janelle's intelligence, and conversation always flowed easily between us.

Janelle has always been career-minded. When I first met her, she worked in marketing communications, but then she switched to human resources at an employment agency. I always seemed to be working transitory jobs—Meri and I were still living our carefree existence and hadn't settled on a logical career path.

After Meri and I had been married for three months, I went looking for a new job. I went to the employment agency where Janelle worked. She helped me out, first with a few part-time positions, and eventually with a full-time job in sales. One afternoon I had to stop by Janelle's office to pick up a check. I passed by her desk to say hello. A quick hello turned into a long conversation. Janelle was very forthcoming about her life. She complained about the guys she was dating, about how immature and unsatisfactory they were. Immediately a thought popped into my head: *Janelle should marry a guy like me*. I thought I was the perfect solution to Janelle's problem. Back then I was young and arrogant. I was also naive. I thought that I was everything Janelle was looking for.

A few months later, Meri and I were getting ready to move from Utah to Wyoming to be close to my family. Meri, Janelle, and I had spent some time together and gotten to know one another even better. In fact, Meri and I were even renting Janelle's old house for a while. I wanted to see Janelle once more before we moved away, so I invited her to lunch with me. Technically, it's inappropriate for a married man to have lunch alone with another woman. But Janelle and I were friends. There was no thought of courting, so lunch was purely platonic.

But during that lunch, that same thought that I'd had a few months earlier in Janelle's office crossed my mind—there was something between Janelle and me. I was a married man, so I had to be careful with my words. I tried to be as offhand as possible when I said to Janelle, "Maybe you and I should consider you and me."

Janelle

I completely rebuffed Kody's suggestion. I was shocked, and laughed it off. After that, I didn't even give it a second thought. But when I returned to the office that afternoon, my coworkers were suspicious. They wanted to know who the cute man was who'd taken me to lunch. I've heard that people in the office said I was glowing—but this seems a little exaggerated.

A few months after Kody and Meri had moved to Montana, Kody told me they were going to be returning to his dad's ranch in Wyoming for the weekend, so I decided to visit as well. When I called my mother and told her I was going to spend a few days with a polygamous family, she became alarmed. Unfortunately, many members of the LDS church harbor a deep mistrust of polygamy. Mormons are taught from a young age that fundamentalism is backward and sinful. I guess my mother was worried that I was going to be converted, swept away into some sort of cult and never heard from again.

Although it was clear that my mom didn't want me to go to Wyoming, she knew me well enough not to tell me *not* to do something. Had she tried to prevent me from visiting Kody and Meri, I would have left the moment I'd hung up the phone.

Ever since my mother divorced my stepfather, she had developed an independent and free spirit. She follows her own path at her own speed. So when I told her I was going to visit Meri and Kody, she told me that she was coming along for the weekend. Part of her wanted to meet a polygamous family and see what they were like—and part of her wanted to protect me from them.

Well, let's just say that trip had an unexpected development. When Kody's father, Winn, arrived and met my mother, they had an instant chemistry. Winn already had two wives, but he and my mom began courting, and not long after our trip to Wyoming they were married.

When I returned to Utah, I began to explore the polygamous faith. There was something in the doctrines that intrigued me. All the men whom I'd met in the faith had character. In addition to this, I discovered that the women were amazingly strong. It became immediately apparent to me that when you choose to follow a countercultural path, you have to learn to be independent. In other words, when you choose an alternative lifestyle— one that is denigrated by the public—it develops your character. You either wash out or you stand up. Once I came to this conclusion, I started to believe that there was something for me in fundamentalism.

As I was investigating the faith, I started studying the doctrines and principles of Meri and Kody's group, as well as talking to a lot of members of their church. I decided to pay another visit to Meri and Kody, who were now living in Montana. When I went up to Montana, I brought the man I was seeing at the time. Despite dating a member of the LDS faith—a conventional Mormon— I couldn't suppress my interest in fundamentalism. During that visit to Montana, it progressed from a curiosity to a calling.

Kody

When Janelle showed up in Montana, she had a guy in tow. I knew she was hoping that a real relationship would develop between them, but I guess I was starting to wish for the opposite to happen. It may be ungenerous to say, but I hoped their relationship would fizzle.

When I saw Janelle and her boyfriend, I couldn't stop wondering why she was sabotaging herself. Don't get me wrong—the boyfriend was an awesome guy. But I had a sense that Janelle and I shared a destiny.

The minute I met Janelle's date, I said to Meri, "She's getting in her own way. She doesn't want to let herself have what she truly wants, so she's dating another guy." I'm not sure Meri quite understood what I was hinting at.

I couldn't shake my spiritual awareness that Janelle and I would one day marry. I'm not sure exactly when this insight came to me—it wasn't born out of the same conventionally romantic attraction I had to Meri. It was a different feeling entirely, one that had more to do with spirituality and intellectual compatibility romantic love. However, I couldn't help notice that in addition to her first-rate mind, I found her extremely attractive.

Since I couldn't shake the awareness that we would share a future, I was confounded by the fact that Janelle brought a date when she came to visit. I was certain that she was doing this to keep herself at a distance from me. In essence, I think she was testing both of our resolves.

Janelle

When I left Montana, I was inspired but confused. I was attracted to the fundamentalist Mormon religion and I was starting to think Kody might be the right person for me. For the first time, I allowed myself the luxury of admitting that I was interested in Kody. Not in a saccharine, gushy romantic way, but because he was emblematic of all the things that attracted me to his faith. But still, I was nervous. Converting to fundamentalism meant leaving my own faith. I needed time to think things through.

I wanted to do some self-exploration. I was only twenty-two, but already I'd been through a divorce. I wanted to get in touch with my own spirituality and my own ideals before making any major decisions. I wanted to travel, to get away from familiar surroundings. Part of me wanted to buy a Jeep, get a dog, and drive off to Colorado and live in the mountains. Another part wanted to explore my interest in the Native American way of life, something that has fascinated me since I was a little girl.

I have always been involved with Native American culture on some level—whether through reading and studying, or through collecting art and artifacts. Many of my friends were involved in the mountain men movement. They participated in reenactments of historical mountain men rendezvous, including spending time living in primitive housing, including teepees. They also practiced many of the crafts, such as furniture making and handiwork, typical of the early 1800s. I decided it would be a good idea to spend some time living closer to nature, as Native Americans once had. I bought a teepee and quit my job, intending to camp in my teepee for as long as I could bear it.

Kody's father had lots of open space on his ranch, and offered to let me camp on his land. By this time, he had married my mother. I knew that if I got too cold in the teepee, I could retreat to a warm house where my mother would be waiting.

I got to Wyoming in November. Cold weather had settled in a while back. And the temperatures in Wyoming are biting and unbearable. Despite this, I was determined. It was below freezing when I got my camp set up. I didn't last a single night. It was so cold that after only a few hours I was back in the house.

I had quit my job in Utah, so I was free to travel up to Wyoming as much as I wanted. Kody's father is a patriarchal man, in the sense that he feels it is his duty and responsibility to look after the people in his family orbit. I was one of these people. He took me under his wing and made it clear that it was his intention to find me a guy. Winn's plan was to convince me to settle on Kody's brother. But I had other ideas.

When I was growing up there was an incredibly cool father in my neighborhood. Perhaps because my stepfather was so distant, I took notice of how closely this man connected to his kids. He was a lawyer, but he would ditch work to take his children skiing. It seemed to me that every moment he was home, he was involved in some activity with one of his kids. It was clear that his children were the center of his world. I remembering thinking how badly I wanted a dad like that.

I'd seen the way Kody interacted with children—there were always kids around the ranch, and Meri's parents' house was often filled with them. I'd seen how loving Kody was and how much fun he could be. He even made time for kids not in his own family. He was energetic and caring, always willing to get down on all fours for any game the kids dreamed up. Kody seemed like exactly the father I had in mind for my kids.

More than anything, I had fallen in love with the polygamous lifestyle. I loved the idea of a sisterhood, the notion of companionship, and the possibility of a family that could grow in so many different ways. I saw so much potential in polygamy.

Kody was an obvious choice for me, but not because of any conventional notion of romance. I have never, ever been someone who's interested in sappy goo-goo eyes, chocolates, flowers, and sunset walks on the beach. The idea of cooing and cuddling doesn't agree with me.

I'm sure there is a combination of things in my nature that makes me think this way. On the one hand, I've always been independent and happy to spend time on my own and do my own thing, so I had never felt the need to bind myself to someone on an intimate level. In addition to this, I think my early failed marriage disillusioned me somewhat, solidifying my notion of matrimony as something both pragmatic and practical. I wanted a strong husband who would be a wonderful father to my children—I always envisioned that I'd have a large number of children. I wanted a man with whom I'd have an intellectual connection, who would be happy and willing to have long discussions with me. I wanted a companion, a friend—and if I found these things in a man, I was certain intimacy would develop from that.

Even though Kody was quite young, he was the most emotionally intelligent man I knew. He was leap years ahead of all the other guys his age. He was the best guy I knew in the polygamous lifestyle I'd become infatuated with. So why wouldn't I want to marry the best guy out there?

Kody

After Janelle's experiment with the teepee, she visited regularly. Meri and I were living in Montana and Janelle sometimes stayed over at our place. One evening, after the three of us had spent the day together, just as we were getting ready for bed, Janelle made an unusual request. "Meri," she said, "can I have a moment alone with Kody so that I can talk to him about something important?"

I suspected what was coming, but Janelle was going about it strangely. She was still in her cowboys and Indians phase—that night she was dressed like a cowgirl in jeans and a khaki corduroy shirt, her hair pulled into a high ponytail.

At the time, Meri and I were living in a cabin with a giant living room and two small, unpleasant bedrooms. Meri went to bed, leaving me and Janelle sitting on the junky furniture I'd picked up at a yard sale.

Janelle was forthcoming. "I think I belong in your family," she said.

I was flattered and pleased, not to mention relieved. Months earlier I had told Meri about my interest in a relationship with Janelle—but it was more of an impromptu suggestion than a serious proposal. So it felt proper that Janelle should make the official opening move. In many ways, it's more appropriate. After all, I was a married man. I should not be making moves on women. That would defile my relationship with Meri.

Quite often in our faith, it's the woman who approaches the family she is interested in. I think people are surprised by how often the woman makes the opening move. If a woman finds a family to which she feels spiritually connected, typically she builds a relationship with the first wife or wives, then she will tell her father, who then speaks to the father of the husband in the family. Now, Janelle didn't exactly play by the rules, but since my father had been involved in trying to find her a husband, it seemed appropriate enough.

Ever since Meri and I got engaged, we had affirmed our commitment to the principle of plural marriage. There are many couples who are polygamous in belief, but live monogamously—in other words, while they believe the principle, they don't live the principle and never take other wives into their families. Meri and I did not want to be one of those couples. We both felt that we'd been called to open our family to additional wives. We'd been married for three years and had three wonderful years of monogamy.

If Meri had misgivings about Janelle, she didn't voice them to me. She seemed happy enough to welcome Janelle into our home. Back then, we were still very young and didn't have the wisdom or the vocabulary to talk about our deepest emotions. So if something was troubling her, I fear she would have been unable to express it in a way I understood.

Meri and I moved back to Wyoming to get ready to bring Janelle into our family. We had to find a house that was big enough for all of us. Janelle and I were officially courting, but things were moving quickly. For various reasons, courtships for second and third wives are traditionally quite short. The most important of these is that it's neither appropriate for a married man to be spending excessive time with a woman who is not his wife, nor is it fair to the other wives to sit at home during a long courtship.

Even in comparison to most plural courtships, Janelle's and mine was particularly short. We managed to go on only one date. And it wasn't much of a date. It took place sometime after New Year's and it was freezing cold. I had been working a fifteen-hour shift, so when I finally got off work, it was late. The town where Meri and I were living in Wyoming was really small. By the time I picked Janelle up, all the restaurants were closed. So we drove around in the dark. Janelle's mother had given me a ring that had been hers. I put the ring on Janelle's finger and asked her to marry me. It was more of a formality than an actual proposal. It was dark, it was late, and it was cold.

Two weeks later we got married. We had a spiritual ceremony on another bitterly cold January night. Then we went on our honeymoon. We had no plan. We just drove and drove, staying wherever we felt like stopping.

Janelle

Except for that brief car ride during which Kody proposed, until our honeymoon, the only time we'd been alone was when we went out to retrieve something from the cow pen on the ranch. Although I was looking forward to finally having the freedom to be alone together, it was awkward at first.

Our courtship had been chaste. We'd only shared one kiss

and it was a very innocent one—when a man is married it's extremely inappropriate to have any physical intimacy during a
courtship.

During the first few days of our honeymoon, it was difficult
for me to consider our relationship as a married couple. Even
though we'd had the spiritual ceremony, which committed us to
each other in a newer, deeper way, I felt no closer to Kody than I
had a week earlier. We had been friends, but now we had to learn
to be husband and wife.

I know now that Kody and I weren't in love then. But there
wasn't a moment that I didn't believe I'd made the right decision,
not just about Kody, but about my new faith.

When I announced my intention to convert from LDS to fundamentalism, I was challenged by many members of my family.
They believed I was not just making a mistake but committing a
sin. Nevertheless, I never once wavered in my decision to accept
the beliefs of my new religion. In marrying Kody, I alienated my
maternal grandparents and my paternal grandmother. My sister,
too, initially rebuffed me. Although it was hard for me to come to
terms with my estrangement from certain members of my family,
I imagined that I'd have sister wives who would, at least in part,
compensate for that loss.

I'm sure all of this was on my mind during my honeymoon.
So I felt pressure for my marriage to succeed right from the start.
However, I had no idea how to go about this. Kody and I had a
deep friendship and we were completely compatible on an in-
tellectual level. We were committed to the decision we'd made.
Now we had to find a way to make it work.

By the end of the honeymoon, we had arrived at a point
where we felt safer with each other. But it would be many, many
years into our marriage before our true love story would begin.

I didn't know when I married Kody what a struggle that first year would be. I moved into the house with him and Meri and lived in their guest room. I felt like a long-term visitor, an eternal houseguest instead of a wife.

Meri and Kody were still very much in love and they had no idea how to incorporate me into their lives. I had no idea where I fit into the marriage. When we watched movies they would sit on the couch and hold hands under a blanket and I'd sit in my own chair.

I didn't feel as if I had my own place in the house. Arguments would erupt over the smallest things—the right way to fold clothes, the right way to clean the kitchen. I felt challenged and confronted on all fronts. I lost my sense of self. I would have to learn to speak up for myself and establish my own life and status within our household.

It wasn't until Kody married for the third time that things would begin to settle down in our household.

Chapter Three
CHRISTINE AND KODY

Christine

I was raised in a polygamous family just outside of Salt Lake. My grandfather was the head of our church, which means my family has been closely involved with all aspects of our faith since I can remember. You could say that when it comes to our church, I'm connected.

Although I was raised polygamous, it wasn't until I was seventeen that I decided, without a doubt, that I was going to accept the principle of plural marriage. It took me a while to come to this decision. I reflected and prayed and turned inward until I had my answer. Eventually, I developed a strong testimony about the way I wanted to live my life.

The biggest influence on my decision to live the principle of plural marriage was my grandmother. She loved having sister wives and knew that the strongest relationship in her marriage was with them. When I decided that I was going to enter into a plural marriage, I knew that it would be only as a third wife. Even as a teenager, I was certain this was the path for me.

I understand how many people might think this is a strange preference. Why would I want to come third when I could come first? But when you think about it, if you are as committed to plural marriage from a young age as I was, you're less interested in the monogamous stage of the relationship than in the plural stage. I wanted sister wives as much as I wanted a husband.

It's a common misconception—at least in my worldview—that it's best to enter a family as first wife. People often think, incorrectly, that the first wife has the highest status and the most security. I never saw it this way. In fact, in my opinion, being the first wife takes too much work and involves too much self-sacrifice. You have to give up your life entirely and be joined at the hip to your husband. It's just you and your husband until the day he marries a second wife. This kind of single-minded devotion never appealed to me—I'm independent and I like my freedom.

Being the second wife didn't seem like a better option either. In fact, I think that would have been worse than being the first wife. The second wife has the hardest job and is put in the most uncomfortable position, because she's the one who comes along and disrupts the marriage of the first wife and her husband. You can't blame her—it's not the second wife's fault. It's just the nature of her role. She's the wedge that comes between the couple. And I was never going to put myself in that position. No matter how fair and understanding a first wife is, there's no way to avoid the emotional struggles and heartache when a second wife joins the family.

But the third wife—she's the lucky one! She's the one who comes along and makes peace between the first two wives. The third wife is in a blessed position. She doesn't have to face marriage on her own without the help from sister wives or bear the burden of breaking up a previously monogamous couple. I was going to be a third wife all the way!

Around my nineteenth birthday, my sister Wendy went on a survival trek with our church. The leaders of her group were a newlywed couple, Meri and Kody Brown. When Wendy returned from her adventure, all she could talk about was Kody. Kody, Kody, Kody! She was full of stories about how strong and athletic Kody was. "Kody pulled us all up a hill!" she said. "He threw us over a wall one by one!"

Wendy explained that Kody and Meri were new to our group, which is why I'd never heard of them before. (As it turned out, Meri had been a member for years—she'd even been over to my house on several occasions, but no one had noticed her until she married Kody.)

The next day, I went to church with Wendy. The hall was crowded. I was checking out the crowd when my eyes landed on a handsome young man. Without my sister telling me, I knew he was Kody. I thought, Wow, Wendy forgot to mention how cute Kody is. He's really, really cute!

Kody

I have to admit that I don't remember seeing Christine in church that morning. I had been in the church for only six months, so the group was fairly new to me. There were different faces at church each week, which made it difficult for me to remember everyone I met.

A week after I returned from the survival trek, our church held a dance. Of course, I attended with my new wife, Meri. (Although I'd met Janelle once or twice, we were only casual acquaintances at this point.) But there was one girl who caught my eye—Christine. She was wearing a turquoise dress with a lace ruffle at the collar. She was bubbly and sweet and as cute as anyone I'd ever seen before. She was also overflowing with positivity. Her liveliness and good cheer were infectious. However, I was still a newlywed and new to the polygamous faith. Although I thought Christine was really cute, I wasn't yet ready to consider a second wife.

I didn't know this, but Christine had a crush on another boy that night. She was just nineteen and she was a romantic. But there was an undeniable spark between us. When I looked at her, I had a feeling—call it a sixth sense—that our destinies were interlaced.

Meri and I didn't have any newlywed friends. And since we didn't have any children and Meri wasn't pregnant, we spent most of our time with single people our age. We always had a group at our house eating ice cream and hanging out. Christine had a big circle of friends, and she always seemed to be in our midst. And since Christine's family was so involved in our church, they regularly hosted gatherings to which Meri and I were usually invited.

While I had an inkling that perhaps something important was starting to develop with Christine—I was awed with how adorable and upbeat she was—Meri and I weren't yet looking to add to our family. We were newlyweds and still very much a couple in love. This made it difficult for me to hang out with my buddies, because it would mean leaving her alone. Eventually, Christine and Meri became friends, which was great. But when I started to notice that Christine was growing interested in me, and when I started visualizing a future together, I knew that exploring this would be unfair to Meri at this point. If Christine and I started hanging out alone—in essence, if we were to start courting— Meri would be abandoned by her two closest friends.

Meri had inadvertently made it clear to me on several occasions that she wasn't prepared to court Christine. One weekend at a field day for the younger members of our faith, I was busy being my loud, boisterous self. I was running all over the field we were gathered at, hosing people down with water. Everybody

was chasing me in order to pay me back. But they couldn't catch me. In the middle of all this, I heard Christine cry out, "Kody, my masculine man!"

I looked over at Meri and I could almost hear her growling. I hadn't seen many examples of plural marriage since I was new to the faith, so this was the first time I experienced it close up. But I couldn't blame her. We were very young.

Despite our initial resistance, something was pulling us together. I couldn't deny that Christine would be part of my family someday, but we all needed to grow up first.

Christine

I loved Kody and Meri, and although my crush on Kody was getting serious, I wasn't interested in marriage yet. Still, I was always eager to hang out with them. Whenever my parents hosted a volleyball party, Meri and Kody always topped the guest list. After spirituality and faith, the trait my dad values most is athleticism, so he was taken with Kody from the start. Whenever I talked to my dad about boys I was interested in, he always steered the conversation in the same direction. "And how is Kody?" he'd ask.

Kody made a big splash when he joined our faith. He was nice looking—which impressed a lot of the women—but he was also well spoken and outspoken. He was confident when he talked in front of a crowd. He knew how to take a spiritual concept and deliver it in a positive and inspiring way. He made a good impression on the people in charge of our church and was often called upon to speak at fireside meetings.

About a year after I first met Kody and Meri, Kody organized a youth trip up to his parents' ranch in Wyoming. Kody wanted to

expose his younger peers to his parents' lifestyle and introduce his parents to young people in their new faith.

By this time it was pretty clear that I had developed a serious crush on Kody. I was always hanging around Meri and him. So when we all piled in our caravan of cars to drive to Wyoming, I got someone to drive my car, and I made sure that I rode in Kody's.

Nineteen people headed up to the ranch for the weekend. We set off from my house in Utah, but when we hit the mountain passes, we drove into a massive snowstorm. It was unbelievably slow going and we had to stop and take turns pushing one another's cars.

The drive should have taken half a day, but we wound up being on the road overnight because of the weather. Since we were all young, it was still fun being out there together. It felt like an adventure.

Kody

We drove all night to Wyoming. It was dangerous. Meri and I rode in the front seat and Christine sat in the back. I kept looking at Christine in the rearview mirror. For months, I'd been watching her. I loved her spark, her bubbliness. She was so full of life and enthusiasm—just the perfect person to have along on a miserable drive. In fact, I was discovering that Christine was the kind of person I wanted to have around all the time. She lit up every room and brought a fun, positive energy to any event. Meri often stood on the sidelines during games and group activities. But Christine was always willing to participate in anything, no matter how silly.

When we set out on our road trip, I was convinced that

Christine was the cutest girl in the world, although she was a little chubby. Back then, I was young and superficial enough to care about physical appearances. After we'd been on the road all night, we stopped at a gas station. I'd been drinking soda pop to stay awake and my stomach felt sour and upset. Just thinking about food made me queasy.

Christine went into the Quickie Mart and bought herself what seemed looked like the largest portion of chili cheese nachos that I'd ever seen. The sight of those nachos turned my stomach. I couldn't watch her eat them. She must have been starving, because she was eating so quickly, and there was chili sauce and nacho cheese everywhere.

Looking back, I hate myself for the thoughts I had at that moment, but the sight of this chubby girl in my car devouring chili cheese nachos for breakfast put the brakes on our relationship. It brought out the most superficial and shallowest side of me. I still liked her—in fact, I liked her very much—but the nacho experience cooled my attraction a little—well, a lot.

Christine

Of course, I had no idea that I'd grossed Kody out with my nachos. I was an overweight kid who liked junk food a little too much. And of all the junk foods in the world, chili cheese nachos were my favorite.

When we finally got to the ranch, Kody transformed into a hero. He was a total stud. All the girls on the trip watched him with their mouths wide open, myself included. I'd seen Kody in action back in Utah. I'd seen him display his talents in church, and I'd seen how he transformed himself into the life of every party. But now I was seeing a whole new side of him.

Kody was the complete cowboy. At the ranch, he was instantly in his element. He got right in there and wrangled cows. He worked the fields. He shoveled and cleaned and got down and dirty with all the animals. I was totally impressed. I thought Kody was the coolest guy in the world.

When I got back home, I was gushing about Kody to a friend. She knew that I wanted to be a third wife, so we came up with a plan. She'd marry Kody first and be his second wife. A few months later, I would join them as third wife. I took this plan much more seriously than my friend, who eventually got married to another man.

My visit to Wyoming had made a fantastic impression on me and I was eager to return. I had become very close to Kody's sister, so when she invited me to spend the summer with her at the Browns' ranch, I accepted immediately.

While I was living with the Browns, a local family started to express their interest in our faith. They had a daughter who, on one visit, spotted a picture of Kody. The minute I saw her look at it, I knew she'd be interested in him. I felt very threatened by her—she was beautiful and thin, and I was immediately afraid she'd catch Kody's eye.

A few months after I met her, this girl was invited to come to an event in Utah for the younger members of our faith. Since I was going down, it fell to me to drive her and to introduce her to some of my friends. Not doing so would have appeared selfish.

I drove the new girl and her brothers to Utah. The whole ride down I kept saying to myself, "What are you doing, you idiot?" I was completely threatened by her. When I got to the youth event, I immediately realized that all my fears were well founded! Right away, Kody and Meri took particular notice of her. Their interest was overwhelming and undeniable. I was heartbroken and jealous, tortured by the fact that Kody seemed to find her more attractive than me. To make things worse, she and Meri

hit it off immediately. They became inseparable—instantaneous best friends.

One morning after I returned from the ranch, Kody and Meri came to pick me up. We'd made plans to spend the day together in the city. Before we left, we lingered on the porch of my parents' house. Kody and Meri had strange looks on their faces—they seemed excited, but a little nervous. Then they told me that they were courting the girl I'd introduced them to at the youth conference.

I was devastated. It ruined my day. In fact, it ruined my year. I decided then and there that I was not going to marry Kody, no matter what happened. It wasn't because of Kody. It was because of the girl he and Meri were courting. She was too young and too cute. And I just couldn't see her in my future. I broke off the friendship. I couldn't be around Kody and Meri while they were courting someone else.

Kody and Meri's news was not the most devastating blow I received that year—not by a long shot. A few months after I returned to Utah, my parents told me they were getting a divorce. Even worse, my mother had decided to leave our faith, which felt like the worst kind of abandonment. I was stunned and inconsolable. I felt as if my world was disintegrating. I'd seen no signs of trouble between my parents and I couldn't imagine a life in which we would no longer be a cohesive family.

I completely shut down. I didn't want anything to do with any of my old friends. I couldn't bear associating with people in Kody's circle or people who'd known my family when it was intact.

I turned inward. I told my father that I wasn't interested in dating and that if a boy approached him and expressed interest in me, I didn't want to know about it. I was so shaken by my parents' divorce that I wanted to make sure I was solid in my faith before I committed myself to someone else. Naturally, I questioned the whole concept of marriage. If my parents couldn't sustain their relationship, what chance did I have when the time came?

Even though I'd cut myself off from a lot of my friends, Meri and I still talked on the phone from time to time. I resisted these phone calls because I didn't want to hear about the courtship. It had been prolonged because Kody and Meri wanted to wait for the girl they were courting to turn eighteen before making their engagement official. Even though I wanted nothing to do with it, I heard when they got engaged, and I knew when they set the date for the wedding.

A week before the wedding, I received a phone call. I was standing in the kitchen when I answered the phone. It was Meri on the other end of the line. My heart nearly exploded with joy when Meri explained that the wedding had been called off. It was the happiest day of my life. I felt as if I could re-enter the world again. I immediately welcomed Kody and Meri back.

But my happiness was short-lived. One day, completely out of the blue, Kody called me up.

"Christine," he said. "Janelle is driving me crazy. I can't stand it. She really frustrates me."

"Who is Janelle?" I said. I had no idea who he was talking about.

"You know her," Kody said. "You've met her here and there."

I had no idea why Kody was bringing this problem to me. Anyway, there was a simple solution. If this woman Janelle was making Kody crazy, wouldn't the easiest thing to do be to stop associating with her?

How wrong I was! The next thing I knew, he and Meri had married Janelle. Of course, I thought this was really weird because Kody had told me that she was driving him crazy. It took me a while to realize what kind of crazy Kody had meant.

After Janelle joined their family, they moved to Wyoming. I had just let Kody and Meri back into my life and now they had moved away with another wife. I hadn't just lost a man who was special to me—I'd lost my best friends.

Kody

After I married Janelle, we traveled down to Utah for a weekend to visit Meri's parents. While we were there, we invited Christine over for dinner. I was used to the gregarious, bubbly Christine. But when she showed up that evening, I immediately sensed an underlying sadness and turmoil within her. It made me sad to see her struggling.

On her way out the door, I pulled her aside. We stepped out on the porch so we could chat. Then I asked her what was wrong.

"Nothing. Everything's fine," she said.

I knew she wasn't telling the truth, and I told her so. I insisted that she tell me what was going on—she was my friend, I loved her, and I needed to know what was breaking her heart.

"It's my parents' divorce," she said. This admission opened up the floodgates, and suddenly Christine felt that she could be open and honest with me once more. I felt the old spark that had always been between us ignite again.

"You know, Christine," I said, "this ordeal may help you in the future. It will make you stronger and more self-aware. And one day you're going to marry a man who is going to appreciate that you've been through something like this and that you have survived it."

I didn't tell her at the time, but I had a feeling that the man she would marry was going to be me.

Christine

Kody really knew how to break my heart. When he told me that one day I'd marry a man who'd appreciate my strength, I was distraught. It seemed that he was implying that he was not going be the man in my future.

Even though I was devastated, I was still more than a little smitten. That night when Kody left, I stood at the door to Meri's parents' house and said good-bye.

"It's not *good-bye*," Kody said. "It's au revoir." Even though Kody's line was cheesy, it sent a current of electricity down my spine. He was flirting with me! Kody shut the door and walked down the steps with Meri toward their car, leaving me inside.

Meri's family immediately sensed what had passed between Kody and me. They all gave me knowing looks. Their faces were warm and inviting, as if they were giving me and Kody their approval. Meri's family's encouragement was too much for me. I believe I gave a small fist pump of joy, then swooned on the couch. I have always been a little dramatic! I knew that no matter what he said, Kody was still the one for me.

A few months later, Kody and Meri came down to Utah for the New Year's ball at our church. Kody asked me to dance over and over and over. I was giddy and could barely keep my feet on the floor. It was the best night of my life. I felt as if I was glittering and glowing.

Right after New Year's, I got a phone call from Meri saying she was planning a surprise party for Kody in Wyoming. She wanted to know if I would bring a group of friends up from Utah. Naturally, I was delighted. I simply couldn't wait to see Kody again.

When Kody walked into the room for his surprise party and saw a bunch of us gathered there, his eyes locked on mine. I knew then how he felt. It gave me courage. The next day we found ourselves alone for the first time. We were sitting on the couch and I just came out with it. "Of all the guys I know, you are the one I'd want to marry."

I was proud of myself for being so forthcoming and honest. Meri's sister Teresa and I drove back to Utah that night. We giggled the entire ride about my future with Kody. When I got back home, I immediately approached my grandfather, who was the head of our church. "Should Kody Brown ask," I said, "tell him that the answer is yes. Let him know that I definitely want to be part of his family."

Kody

Christine really made it easy for me to get permission to court her. When I called her dad, he was thrilled. "This is great, Kody. This is great," he said. It was exactly what he'd been hoping for.

Christine's father was aware of how she glowed when we were together. He was also aware of how she had pushed all other boys to the sidelines in favor of me. He wanted her to be happy. And now he knew that she made me happy. "Christine just loves you," her father said.

His only question for me was regarding my loyalty to our church. In his mind, this single question determines worthiness. Since the day I converted, my faith has never wavered, not for a single second. I told him that, and he was convinced.

On Valentine's Day, I asked Meri's sister Teresa, who lived in Utah near Christine, to buy a bouquet of roses. I instructed her to write, "Let's get the ball rolling," on the card. Teresa offered to deliver the roses to Christine at work. Christine was a title clerk at a car dealership. The whole office knew that she was from a polygamous family. In fact, they knew that she had a crush on me, a man with two wives. It's a testament to Christine's outgoing nature and wonderful personality that people do not judge her for her beliefs.

It turns out that the day I asked Teresa to send Christine flowers, Christine had called in sick to work. But by some wonderful coincidence, she had called Teresa to tell her that she was unwell and would be staying home, so Teresa knew where to deliver the roses.

That night I called Christine. We were both overjoyed and a little giddy. The following weekend, Janelle and I traveled down to Utah. Janelle generously offered to hang out with some people in our church so that I could have some time alone with Christine.

Janelle was very sweet and accepting of my courtship with Christine. I knew that things were difficult between her and Meri in the house, and I believed she was hoping for a new sister wife to be her ally or friend. Meri was slightly more prickly when I started courting Christine. However, she liked Christine and was aware of how close the two of us were. I'm sure as far as Meri was concerned, bringing Christine into the family was just a matter of time.

Christine and I spent as much time together as possible that weekend. It wasn't what I'd call romantic—Christine was quite puritanical in her view of romance and courtship—but we had fun. I think we held hands and maybe hugged once or twice, but that was the extent of it. That weekend we got engaged.

I wanted to prolong our engagement, but Christine didn't want to. She insisted on setting a wedding date as quickly as possible. She believed that a long courtship would be inappropriate and unfair on her new sister wives. She didn't want to be running around with a married man. I tried telling her that I wasn't quite ready, but Christine felt that she'd already waited so long—

we'd been friends for three years. We decided to get married in six weeks.

The minute I asked Christine to marry me, I realized that I had once again acted too quickly. I was in over my head. I was not even twenty-five, I already had two wives, and Janelle was expecting our first child. The thought of trying to bring Christine into our family gave me serious pause. I'm afraid I showed up at our wedding with what Christine calls a "thousand-yard stare." Suddenly, I felt the weight of the world on my shoulders. I was nervous and apprehensive.

I knew there was a lot about my life that Christine didn't understand. She had only ever seen me as the life of the party and the good-time guy. She didn't know how tense things were between Meri and Janelle, and hadn't had much opportunity to get to know them herself. When I proposed, I was working at a job that was crushing my soul. Meri and Janelle were miserable with each other and I didn't know how to negotiate a truce between them. And now I was introducing a third wife into an unstable environment. I had no doubt that Christine was the right person, but I sensed it was too early to marry her.

All of this was running through my head as I joined Christine in marriage. What I didn't know then was that Christine would become a major factor in our success as a family. Her kindness and her positive nature brokered a peace in our household. Christine saved our bacon, as I like to say. She saved the Browns. But back then, all I could see were the struggles that lay ahead.

I worked right up until the day we got married. I even had a hard time getting off work to attend my own wedding. Christine had to organize the whole wedding herself. Neither my father nor Christine's mother attended the ceremony. It was a hard day for us. I didn't have time to plan a honeymoon. In fact, it didn't even occur to me to plan one. No one told me that I should. When I wasn't buried in my work, I was a Ping-Pong ball bouncing between two wives who always had their bristles up. Obviously, they weren't interested in advising me on what I should do with Christine.

After our wedding, Christine and I got in the car and drove to Montana. It was a tense trip, and I have to admit that I wasn't my most cheerful self. Christine and I had gone from being buddies to being married. We hadn't had time to get used to each other and I hadn't prepared myself for the transition of adding a new wife to my family.

Christine

I was shaken when Kody showed up at our wedding with that look on his face. He was morose. I was even more devastated when I learned that he hadn't planned a honeymoon. I was hoping that we'd finally have a romantic getaway, something special that told me how thrilled he was to have me in his family. I was young and naive. I had no idea how to tell Kody what I wanted from him.

On our honeymoon—a drive through the sticks of Montana—I was struck by the realization that I didn't know Kody very well. Once we got into the car, he still had the faraway look on his face that I'd seen at our wedding. He seemed distant and unreachable. I began to understand that he felt overwhelmed. However, I didn't know how to talk to him about what he was feeling. I had no idea how to reach out to him. I just sat there in silence.

Watching him drive with that look on his face made me unbearably sad. I realized that I had no idea how to express my feeling with him or ask him to share his with me. I never doubted that Kody was the man of my dreams, but I began to worry that I'd married him too soon.

Until our honeymoon, I had thought he was a fun-loving guy, but that was the extent of it. Now there was this distant, grumpy man at my side, burdened by something I couldn't understand. And I worried that I might be the source of his anxiety. Like many young women, I had idealized marriage. I had this silly notion that the moment you got married, your problems ended. I was fixated on the idea of happily ever after. I thought marriage, especially plural marriage, would be absolute bliss. What could be better than being blessed with a husband and sisters in one fell swoop?

I didn't understand that marriage is something you must work on. I didn't know that true love isn't instantaneous but something that develops over time. While Kody and I did love each other, it took us about a year from the day we married to fall completely head over heels for each other. It would be a hard year, but well worth the wait.

Chapter Four

ROBYN AND KODY

Robyn

I was raised in a polygamous family in southern Utah. My mother was my father's second wife. They had a truly wonderful marriage—a honeymoon experience that lasted for years and years. Their relationship was sweet, loving, and respectful. They put their family and their happiness in front of any petty grievance that might crop up. I was determined not to marry unless I could find the same kind of relationship.

I grew up knowing that accepting the doctrine of plural marriage was entirely up to me. It was something I considered deeply and carefully. I prayed and contemplated until I received a testimony—which is to say, until I knew without question—that I was going to live the principle of plural marriage.

I got married at twenty-one to a fellow member of my faith. He was from a well-regarded family in our community. Despite the fact that my then-husband's family members were spiritual leaders, our marriage was not solid. We struggled right from the start.

I was the first wife, but shortly after my son was born, I knew without a doubt that I wanted to have sister wives. Unfortunately, my marriage didn't last long enough to bring a second wife into our family.

I tried my hardest to make the marriage work, both for our own sake and for the sake of the three children my ex-husband and I had together. But what started off as unstable disintegrated into something destructive. After seven and a half years of marriage, we separated. A year and a half later, we were divorced.

Both my marriage and its collapse were incredibly difficult for me. I suffered a lot of pain and hardship. I had been badly mistreated and misled by my ex-husband. While I knew that he was the source of a lot of my grief, part of me still believed that I was a failure because I hadn't been able to make my relationship work.

The aftermath of my marriage left me feeling vulnerable and used, as well as exposed and helpless. I felt betrayed. I needed to regain my confidence and my inner strength, to ensure that I would never be mistreated again. It took me a while to realize that the only person I could rely on to protect me was *myself*. When I discovered this, I invented an alter ego who became my protector. Her name was She-Rah and she represented my tougher, bolder side. Since no one would come to my rescue, I transformed part of me into my own superhero.

She-Rah helped me protect the softer, more sensitive parts of my psyche. She built a wall around them so they wouldn't be battered or bruised. I knew that it would be going against my nature to throw away the kindness and caring that are important parts of my character—so instead I developed this mechanism to shield them. She-Rah helped me put up a fortress around my vulnerabilities and develop a hard, impenetrable side so that I wouldn't fall for anyone's tricks again.

She-Rah was instrumental is helping me cope with the emotional turmoil caused by my marriage. She was there to ensure that I would never be hurt again. Any man who approached me was going to have to prove himself in every way possible—and he would have to go through She-Rah.

Since both my marriage and my divorce were so difficult, I decided that I would take a break from relationships. I didn't need the complications of dating in my life. I knew that since I was a mother of three, my dates would be more like job interviews than romantic encounters. After all, any man who might court me needed to be up to the task of helping me raise my children. And while I wasn't outwardly considering marriage, I was pretty certain that if it happened, I would join a family as a plural wife.

If and when I married again, I wouldn't care the least bit what my husband looked like. None of the superficial stuff mattered to me anymore. My husband could be old or young, fat or skinny—I didn't care as long as he was a good man and a good husband. I wanted someone whose sole priority was taking care of his family. I knew that anyone who was interested in this job would have to demonstrate himself thoroughly and competently as caring, unselfish, and strong. I wasn't taking any chances. But before I even contemplated marriage or courtship, I was determined to take time out for myself, repair my wounds, and look after my children.

After my divorce was finalized and I was functioning as a single mom, I went to visit my cousin Reba in Lehi, Utah, which is thirty miles outside of Salt Lake. I hadn't been there in a while and I was looking forward to a change of community.

On Sunday, Reba and I went to church. While we were seated in the service, a man sitting in front of me with shaggy blond hair caught my eye. The first thing I noticed about him was his eyes, which were ringed with laugh lines. I always love seeing laugh lines because they tell me that someone is happy. I watched him talk with the other members of the congregation.

There was something peaceful and comforting about the way he conducted himself. He was smiling and laughing, at ease with himself and others. All of a sudden, he looked up and our eyes met. I'm not exaggerating when I say I felt as though I'd been shot through with a bolt of lightning. When this happened, I was stunned. I was embarrassed, too, and looked down at my feet.

Immediately, I was furious that I'd had any sort of response to this stranger. I was determined that no one should break through my hard exterior shell and play with my emotions. So before She-Rah could scold me, I quickly repaired the crack that had appeared in my armor.

Sometime during the service, I had to walk past this man on my way to the bathroom. He was sitting with a group of women. In my bitterness at my own emotional vulnerability, I thought, *He is probably an idiot.* I dismissed the whole encounter entirely.

A month later I visited Reba again. On the afternoon I was getting ready to leave, she had a group of friends over at her house. While I was standing on her front lawn, packing the kids into the car to head home, the same man I'd locked eyes with in church drove up in a white convertible. There was a woman riding in the passenger seat. The man stopped the car and started talking to my cousin. It was like a party exploded out of that car—he was so dynamic and full of energy.

Reba introduced me to Kody Brown and his wife Meri. I fought to suppress the memory of that electric sensation that I'd felt in church a month earlier. She-Rah was screaming at me from inside my head, warning me to not even look at Kody. It was difficult to ignore him—he was so animated and loud—but I did. I focused on Meri instead. She was sweet and engaging.

Eventually Kody noticed that I wasn't part of the small crowd that had gathered around him. So he turned to me and said, "And who is your husband?"

"I don't have one," I said.

Then he teased me about marrying me off to one of the guys sitting around on my cousin's lawn.

I thought nothing of it as I drove off. I imagined that somewhere down the line I might become friends with Meri. But that was as far as my thinking went concerning the Browns.

A few weeks later, my mother started bugging me about attending a church dance back in Lehi. I had no interest in going. I was embarrassed about showing my face as a single woman again, a divorcée. After all, everybody knew my story. I had been married to the son of a very prominent family, so my dirty laundry was public knowledge. It made me uncomfortable. But my mother insisted that I "get my scent out there." I agreed to go to the dance, but only to escort my brother and sister, who needed a social outlet.

When I got to the dance, I felt like an idiot. But my mother was right, at least in part. I needed to put my face out there and show people that I wasn't ashamed. I was validated in the breakup of my marriage and had nothing to hide.

At the dance, I ran into Meri. She immediately rushed over and starting talking to me. She was so friendly and sweet.

"Thank you so much for talking to me," I said. "I feel like such an idiot right now. It's so nice of you to think of me." After a while, Meri returned to Kody and their friends.

When the second to last song of the night came on, Kody asked me to dance. I was shocked. I remember thinking that Meri must have taken pity on me and made her husband dance with me. I felt like a complete loser, but I let Kody have his pity dance, and I thought it was kind of Meri to send him over.

When Kody and I started dancing, we were immediately at ease with each other. I felt relaxed around him. Kody was easy to talk to. Eventually we stopped dancing and stood chatting in the middle of the dance floor. During that song and the next, we opened up to each other like it was the most natural thing in the world. I forgot about the dance, the hall, and all of the people around us. For ten minutes, it felt as if Kody and I were the only people in the world.

All of a sudden Kody said, "Will you excuse me, please?" They were saying a prayer to finish the dance and I hadn't even noticed. I'd completely lost track of time and place. It was as if Kody and I had escaped to an island together. I'd been so involved in our conversation that I'd forgotten where we were.

After the prayer, Kody and Meri came up to my sister and me and started talking. The four of us talked until they kicked us out of the hall. Then we stood on the steps in the dark of the building and talked until two in the morning.

I was curious about Meri and wanted to get to know her better, but she was very quiet. Kody kept engaging my sister in conversation about plural marriage. She was a first wife and was interested in living the principle, which intrigued Kody.

My impression of Kody was that he was a nice, thoughtful, interesting man who liked conversation. After he and Meri left, my sister started teasing me, telling me that she was sure Kody liked me. I told her she had no idea what she was talking about. Then I explained it wouldn't have mattered if Kody had been head over heels for me. I had made an agreement with myself and with God. I was not putting myself out there. I was not available. If God wanted me to marry someone, then He'd have to hit me over the head with it and give me irrefutable proof that this is what I was meant to do. In the meantime, I told my sister, I'm going to figure myself out and get my kids in a safe situation.

The next day I drove home to southern Utah. I assumed I'd never see Kody again.

Kody

After Meri and I met Robyn on the lawn of her cousin's house, Meri instantly sensed that there was something special about Robyn. I was nervous because Robyn was divorced and divorce can bring a lot of technical difficulties in terms of blending families and raising another man's children. I had always declared that I wouldn't invite this situation into my life. But the stirring I felt around Robyn changed this almost right away.

Meri was incredibly excited to run into Robyn at the dance. She acted like a schoolgirl, figuring out how and when I should ask Robyn to dance. The minute Robyn and I hit the dance floor, I became transfixed by her spirit. I couldn't deny the spark I felt—not the kind of spark you feel in your loins, but something deep and transcendent. I guess you could call it love at first sight.

When we were talking after the dance, I went out of my way to avoid flirting with Robyn and focused most of my energy on talking to her sister. By that time, I had a very deep sense that there was a spiritual connection between us, but I didn't want to be overbearing or inappropriate. Eventually, I ended the conversation with Robyn and her sister. I assumed I would see Robyn at church with the main congregation the next day.

When Meri and I got home that night, we stayed up for two more hours talking about Robyn. We rehashed the whole experience at the dance and after. We discussed our feelings about a new wife and whether Robyn would be that person. Robyn's energy really appealed to Meri, and Meri was looking forward to having her as a friend, as well as a potential sister wife.

Despite our minor disagreements, our family was stable. All my wives were happy. Our children were happy. We had arrived at the place we'd be dreaming of since I married Christine. It seemed like an insane idea to threaten the peace in our household by considering a new wife. But both Meri and I were convinced that Robyn had a wonderful spirit—kind and profound. Even our brief conversation with her stirred our souls. We wanted to get to know her better. I felt an undeniable connection to this woman I had just met, as did Meri. This connection was so deep and spiritual that it kept us up all night.

We were lost in our own world as we discussed this undeniable feeling we both shared that Robyn was not just a special person on her own, but a special person to us. Meri and I kept looking into each other's eyes and saying, "Something's happening. We feel something happening."

Before we went to sleep, I climbed out of bed and went to the living room. I fell on my knees and began to pray. I told God that I felt a stirring, and that I wanted to know if this special woman I'd just met belonged in our family.

When I got to church in the morning, Robyn was nowhere to be found. I was crestfallen. I was certain that she was as interested in me as I was in her. It seemed impossible to me that she wouldn't have attended my congregation in the hopes of seeing me again.

I was angry at myself. If I'd known that Robyn wasn't going to be at church the next day, I would have never have been a gentleman and ended our conversation the previous evening. I would have insisted we all go out for pie and stay up as late as possible. During church, Meri texted me to ask if I'd seen Robyn. I told her I hadn't. Meri was as disappointed as I was.

After the service, I saw Robyn's cousin Reba, who had introduced us in the first place. I was still a little giddy from the night before. Since I believed that Robyn and I had a deep connection, there was no way in my mind that our experience could have been one-sided. I was simply convinced that she was as smitten with me as I was with her. So I went up to Reba and said, "Maybe you should call Robyn and ask her who she's thinking about right now." Reba looked baffled.

A week later, Reba told Meri and me that she wanted to come over to our house to talk about what our intentions were regarding Robyn. She was both curious and protective.

Before Reba arrived at our house, Meri grew very emotional. She hugged me and said, "Kody, what if we're not right? What if she's not meant to be with us? What if we're wrong about the way we feel?"

I explained to Meri that what I felt for Robyn was undeniable. The spiritual and emotional connection was not going to be undone by any personal insecurities Meri and I may have had. I told her that this person whom God had brought into our lives was meant to be there. It only had to be ratified by Robyn, her parents, and our church leaders.

When Reba showed up she was very direct. "I have to know what you two are thinking about Robyn," she said.

Meri and I exchanged glances and then explained that we'd both been bitten by the same love bug. We told her that our feelings concerning Robyn were profound. We explained that we fully intended to look into getting to know Robyn better if she was open to it. Reba got a little giddy. She loves Robyn and she loves us. She was excited to see if our families were meant to be together.

Robyn

After my cousin talked to Kody and Meri, she called me and told me I needed to get down to Lehi immediately. This was crazy, since Lehi is three hundred miles from where I lived. I told her she was out of her mind. I had zero intention of coming down and falling in line with her little plan.

"Robyn," Reba said. "This is a good family. They're very interested in you. There are a lot of positive things happening here. You need to come and meet all of them."

"All of them?" I said. "How many are there?"

Reba explained that Kody had three wives.

"Three?" I said. I had already had my testimony that I was going to be part of a plural family. I knew that since I was a divorcée and I was older with kids, I wouldn't be a first wife again. But I'd never even entertained the possibility of being a fourth wife.

The majority of men in our faith have two wives. Fewer have three wives, and hardly any have four. It's just too challenging. So when Reba told me Kody had three wives, I was a little taken aback. It seemed like a lot. Then she informed me that they'd been a family together for sixteen years. It seemed inconceivable that I'd put myself in this situation.

I told Reba, "No. No way. I don't need these complications. Anyway, I can't afford the trip."

But Reba insisted and told me that she would pay for my gas. I still told her no, but I said I would think about it.

For the next couple of days, I contemplated a lot. I asked God to give me a sign, even though I know He doesn't work that way. I played all these little games with myself, for instance, promising that if I saw the name "Kody" written anywhere, I'd take it as a sign that I should go.

Eventually I decided to ask my kids if they wanted to go on this trip—though I didn't explain that it wasn't just to see Reba. It was a long car trip, something they hated. I figured I'd be off the hook. I guess I was looking for an excuse not to go, but to my surprise they said they wanted to! So I agreed.

The whole trip to Lehi, She-Rah was screaming at the top

of her lungs, "Don't do this. Get your butt home. Now!" I had to agree with her. I had no idea what I was doing. She yelled at me until I pulled into my cousin's driveway. I hadn't even gotten out of the car when Reba swooped down on me. "We're going to the Browns'," she said.

Kody

Reba let Meri and me know that she had talked Robyn into coming to Lehi. I was excited and I wanted to put together a barbecue to welcome her. I still hadn't told Janelle about Robyn. I had only seen Robyn a handful of times and I wasn't sure what sort of footing we were on. I wanted to make sure she was at least slightly open to the idea of a relationship with me before I broached the subject with my wives. Naturally, I would need their consent to court her.

I approached Janelle first. I explained what had been going on with Meri, Robyn, and me, and what my feelings were.

When I finished talking, Janelle had a surreal experience. She was overcome with emotion. She put her hand over her chest and said, "Oh my goodness. There's something special about this. This is supposed to happen." Tears welled up in her eyes. She says she felt a burning in her bosom. It was an undeniable affirmation.

I was moved by Janelle's reaction to my news. It made me giddy for Robyn's arrival. I had told Christine about Robyn the night after the dance. Christine expressed her disappointment that she hadn't stayed later to meet her. Christine is such a warm and inviting person, I knew that she would go out of her way to welcome Robyn. Soon I had my wives' consent to get to know Robyn.

I found myself counting down the minutes until Robyn turned up. I was smitten. And I was convinced that Robyn felt the same way about me. I thought that when Robyn arrived at my house, we'd be off to the races.

No such luck. When Robyn came up the stairs and saw me flipping burgers out on the grill, she barely even said hello.

Robyn

I had no idea what to expect when I turned up at the Browns'. The first thing I noticed was that there were three convertibles parked in the driveway. For some reason, I had the impression that they were trying to show off for me. "What is this? An episode of *Cribs*?" I asked Reba.

Later on, to my horror, Reba repeated this to Kody in front of me and added, "Hey, Kody, you want to make it four convertibles?" I wanted to kill her.

When I walked into the large house where all three wives had their own separate apartments, I was nervous and a little overwhelmed. My cousin was parading me around, which is not my style at all. Everybody was staring at me, especially Janelle and Christine, who'd never met me before. Luckily, Meri was friendly and sweet. In fact, she stuck by my side as if she were laying claim to our friendship.

It was uncomfortable to have all these eyes on me. I kept wondering what I was doing there, in the middle of this family. After all, I am not the type of woman who chases married men. During the entire cookout, She-Rah was screaming, "Leave. Get out. Go. This is scary."

Kody says that he felt electricity between us that night, but I was working hard to prevent any connection. I would simply not allow myself to be open in any way. I put up my wall and I hid behind it. However, there was one moment when this wall crumpled completely.

Janelle had left the cookout early and gone to bed because she had to drive to Wyoming the next morning to collect the older children, who were staying on their grandparents' ranch. Many of the younger kids were still running around the backyard. When Janelle said good night, Kody told her that he would put Savanah, their youngest child, to bed a little while later.

I wanted to check on my kids, who were off playing somewhere in the house. The house was big and I had no idea where anything was. I walked through Meri's apartment and spied Kody in the kitchen. He was holding Savanah, washing her feet in the sink.

He didn't know I was watching. I couldn't take my eyes off him as he scrubbed something sticky off of Savanah's feet so she would be clean and comfortable while she slept. The love and care he put into this simple gesture was astounding. No one nagged him to do this. He wasn't trying to impress me. He simply cared enough to make sure that her feet were clean. I was struck by this moment. It broke through the hard, bitter shell that I'd erected around myself. But even as I watched Kody, I reminded myself not to fall for him or for anyone else in that house.

The next day, I met the Browns at Sunday school. Reba and I were talking to Meri, Kody, and Christine, who were very happy to see me. Meri turned to me and asked, "Would you like to come over for lunch? For dinner? Forever?"

I turned beet red. But I agreed to come for lunch.

Later, after church, I found myself back at the Browns' house. Janelle was picking up the older kids. Meri had run an errand, and Christine was bustling in and out. So Kody and I were left pretty much to ourselves. It was awkward. Kody could sense my discomfort and tried teasing me a little. When that didn't work, he tried to dig into my past and find out more about what had led me to my current situation. I told him that I preferred to wait until all his wives were home so I could tell them all at once.

Suddenly, the door opened, and all the teenage kids burst in. They stormed the house. Kody ran up to Logan, his oldest, and hugged him like his best friend. All the kids were talking at once. All the adults were talking at once. Everyone was so happy to see the kids, and the kids were so thrilled to be back home. It was loud and chaotic, but also lovely and remarkable. Everyone was so engaged with one another. It was the most dynamic atmosphere I'd ever encountered.

It was immediately clear to me how much this family loved one another. It hit me exactly how much both my kids and I had been missing out on a thriving, stable family experience. The thing I wanted for my kids first and foremost was a good family. And here it was in front of me, a family literally overflowing with love.

Everyone was all talking at once in what I've come to know as typical Brown style—trying to see who can talk the loudest. (I've learned that there is rarely a quiet moment in the Brown house.) They were all so animated and expressive and full of stories. I felt as if I was looking inside their world. It was an amazing experience. I fell in love with Kody's family before I fell in love with him.

But Kody did impress me. He was everywhere at once. He was meeting kids' needs. He was wiping a nose, picking things up, helping with dishes. He was checking in with his wives. He was going out of his way to make sure everyone was okay.

Kody

Eventually Madison, who was fourteen at the time, noticed Robyn sitting in the corner. "Dad, who is that?" she asked.

For a long time, I'd had a running joke with my kids about taking a young wife. They had agreed that the youngest woman I might marry had to be twenty-eight at least.

"That's Robyn," I said to Madison, "and she's thirty."

Madison picked up on my insinuation right away and immediately she got a twinkle in her eye.

Eventually, Meri, Janelle, Christine, and I sat down with Robyn in Meri's living room. Robyn was very forthcoming and direct. She laid out all that she had been through, explaining about her ex-husband and their destructive relationship. She said that before things went any further, she didn't want there to be any secrets about her kept from the family.

While Robyn was laying it on the line for us, Christine leaned over and got right in her face. "So, do you think our husband is cute or not?"

Robyn didn't know Christine well enough to understand that she was joking. Robyn explained that this sort of decision was left up to God and what He thought was right. Whether or not she thought I was cute was immaterial. She said that she was just there to figure out if this was something that God wanted for her. She was all business.

Her answer took the wind right out of my sails. I'd been hoping she would confess to the same electricity I'd felt when I was with her. I was deflated. Finally, Robyn explained that pursuing a married man isn't something she'd ever do. "Yeah, right, you hussy," Christine teased.

Robyn looked mortified.

By the end of the evening, I was despondent. I was not just

smitten with her, but in love. And I'd believed, incorrectly, that she had similar feelings for me. Now I realized that I'd have to court her affection.

The next day, when I got home from work, I discovered that Meri had invited Robyn over. Since my wives had given me permission to get to know Robyn—which is the first step in approaching a new wife—I decided to say what was on my mind.

"Robyn," I said, "do you want to see if we can get to know each other better?"

"Maybe. But I'm not asking anyone's permission," she said. This meant she wasn't going to approach her father or the church leaders. All the hard work had fallen to me. She was not going to make things easy.

Robyn

There are several ways for a woman to enter a plural marriage. One of these is to tell her father and her church leaders, after which they would approach the family. I felt uncomfortable with this. I was a divorced woman. People were already under the impression that I was hunting for a husband—which was completely untrue. Even though I had legitimate grounds for divorce from my first husband, a failed marriage still tarnished my reputation. So I was especially careful not to give the impression that I was desperate to remarry. I didn't want to chase anyone. Especially because I had three children, to be so bold as to ask about a married man seemed very presumptuous. In our community— and I'm sure others—imagining that a man, especially one with many other children, wants to take responsibility for your kids is taking a lot for granted.

Eventually, Meri convinced Kody to talk to the church leader.

This is an important step in our faith for several reasons, one of which is so the church can make sure that a man has pure intentions and is not simply wife chasing. Kody was uncharacteristically shy about approaching the leader. But when Christine and Meri accompanied him to the meeting, Kody was immediately given permission to talk to my father.

When Kody called my father to ask permission to court me, my father was guarded. He knew how badly I'd been hurt before. "You can't court her, but you can get to know her," my father said. "No flowers, no chocolates, no love letters."

Since I lived so far away from Kody, he and I talked on the phone regularly. Meri and I also kept in contact. Eventually, we started visiting on weekends. Whenever Kody visited me, he brought one of his wives or several of his children so that I could get to know the family better.

During this process, we were very chaste. We never hugged. We only held hands a couple of times, and that was in order to say a prayer. The only time we were alone during the "getting to know each other process" was to get chicken from the grocery store.

Soon, I started to fall in love with him. I felt safe with Kody, and I felt comfortable with his family. Kody did and said everything perfectly. He proved himself to me effortlessly. However, I was still waiting for a "eureka" moment when I'd know without a doubt that I was meant to be part of Kody's family. I wanted fireworks and fanfare. I wanted angels singing in my ears. I wanted a sign from God.

While I was waiting for this to happen, I wanted to deepen my relationship with Kody. So I told my dad, who called Kody and gave him permission to court me at last.

Kody

For a couple of years before I met Robyn, I had been working as a sales representative selling advertising for billboards. While this job allowed me to work locally, it was a tough way to make a living. There were times when I could barely sell at all.

The day that Robyn's father called and gave me permission to court Robyn, my sales career had hit an all-time low. Things were so tough that I was considering selling my car. I didn't have two nickels to rub together, but I was still considering courting this amazing woman. I was certain that God would find a way for me to bring Robyn into my life.

After I got off the phone with Robyn's dad, I told my wives that we'd received permission to court. Luckily, Robyn was visiting Lehi at the time, so we could immediately go on a date. My wives were all excited for me. Each of them had received the answer that Robyn was meant to be in our family. In fact, Christine had received a more intense spiritual witness that Robyn should marry me than she had received about her own marriage. Together we teased Robyn mercilessly about the fact that we all knew her destiny. My wives and I were in what Robyn called the "Knowing Club," while Robyn was still waiting for her answer.

On our first date, over lunch, Robyn and I confessed everything about ourselves to each other—stretch marks, smelly feet, bad habits. We wanted to get all the silly stuff out of the way. When we got back in the car, it had rained slightly and the sky was beautiful with sunlight pushing through the rain clouds. I looked over at Robyn. "I love you," I said. I couldn't help myself. Saying those words was a relief—an absolutely cathartic experience.

Robyn

I may have loved Kody, but I wasn't saying it until I was 100 percent sure. Words can be cheap and I wanted to be careful. Now that we were courting, Kody and I started visiting with each other without the company of his wives. It was time to get to know each other better. I didn't want to be rushed into a marriage and family that was still unfamiliar. I know some people in our faith want a quick courtship and engagement, but I needed to build a better foundation. I didn't want to go to my wedding day and wedding bed with someone who was a relative stranger. In addition to God's testimony, I wanted a romantic love.

Some of my sister wives were more interested in the sisterhood than in the husband. But perhaps since I'd been married before, I knew that I needed a man whom I loved, trusted, cherished, and adored. I also knew that asking for and receiving all these things is hard.

During a visit I made to see Kody, I began to pray and fast in order to receive a sign or an affirmation that I was meant to be in his family. I needed something concrete. I knew I was falling in love with him. I felt him breaking down all of my walls. I felt She-Rah putting away her sword. On one of our dates we drove to Thanksgiving Point, a beautiful lookout where Kody had a billboard he was eager to sell.

On this drive, I had a singular experience. I felt my heart start to swell. It seemed to be growing bigger in my chest. It even hurt. I started to feel out of breath, but also at peace, because I was with Kody and he was wonderful. Suddenly, I felt as if the Heavenly Spirit was talking to me. And I knew. This was my affirmation. I knew without a doubt that this is whom I was meant to marry. I burst into tears. Kody looked at me, wondering what was wrong. Then he began to cry, too. We were both so overcome.

Kody

I had been planning to ask Robyn to marry me on her birthday. But I jumped the gun. A few days before her birthday, she told me that an older and esteemed man in our faith had called to inquire about courting her. This was a shock to my system. I was devastated. I didn't have the money to marry and support Robyn, but I knew that I would have to find a way. Even though Robyn told the man she knew where she belonged, I was still shaken.

The next day, Robyn and I drove back out to Thanksgiving Point. As we sat there talking, I was overcome with what I believed was God's spirit. Before I knew what I was doing, I took her hand and asked her to marry me.

When Christine and I got engaged, she told me she wouldn't kiss me until we were at the altar. After we were married, she realized she had made a mistake and made me promise that if I married again, I'd kiss my next wife before we said our vows. So I took Robyn's face in my hands and kissed her. Robyn leaped out of the car and began to dance around. She was so happy and joyful. I got out of the car, and she jumped into my arms. This happened on September 26. We wouldn't get married for six months. Our lives were in upheaval. I couldn't support Robyn yet. I couldn't even move her to our town—but I knew God would help me do what it would take to bring our families together when the time was right.

Meri and Kody

Janelle and Kody

Christine and Kody

Robyn and Kody

Meri and Kody enjoying the snow.

Janelle and Kody pose against the rocks.

Christine, Kody, Aspyn, and Mykelti taking a road trip.

Robyn and Kody at Plymouth Rock.

Kody holding Aspyn, Mariah, and Madison.

In the tub: Logan, Mariah, Madison, Aspyn, Hunter, Mykelti, and Paedon.

Logan, Mariah, Madison, Aspyn, Hunter, Mykelti, Paedon, Garrison, Gabriel, and Gwendlyn.

Logan, Mariah, Madison, Aspyn, Hunter, Mykelti, Garrison, and Paedon at Christmas.

Meri and Kody with daughter
Mariah in Times Square.

Janelle's kids
(*back to front*):
Madison,
Hunter, Logan,
Savanah, Gabriel,
and Garrison.

Christine's kids
(*back to front*):
Ysabel, Aspyn,
Mykelti,
Paedon, Truely,
and Gwendlyn.

(*Left to right*)
Breanna, Dayton,
Robyn, Solomon,
Kody, and Aurora.

The camera crew relaxing.

Putting reindeer noses on for the camera.

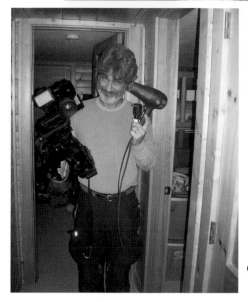

One of the cameramen.

The Brown Family

PART TWO

SORORITY

Chapter Five

MERI

Like many women who choose plural marriage, I idealized the nature of sister wives. I was eager for my first sister wife to be my friend in addition to being married to my husband. I never wanted to be in a situation with a sister wife who didn't want to associate with the rest of the family. As I imagined it, it would be the most natural thing in the world for my sister wives and me to form instantaneous friendships.

Paradoxically, I am reserved but at times can be opinionated, which makes me cautious about quickly forging close relationships with women. In forming friendships and relationships, I need to feel safety and trust with the other person before I feel I can open up to a deep relationship. But when I do, I value them deeply and expect these friendships to last. When Kody and I entered into our first courtship with a young woman we'd been introduced to at a church gathering, I was excited. She and I became close friends right away. This was unusual for me and I immediately took it as a sign that Kody and I were destined to marry her. This girl and I loved hanging out together and spent lots of time on our own without Kody. As I saw it, we were on our way to achieving the sister wife ideal I'd always imagined.

Though sometimes I got jealous of the afternoons she and Kody went off on their own to develop their relationship, I did my best to deal with those feelings maturely. I felt confident that the three of us had a wonderful future together and I was certain that while she would be a great wife to Kody, she would remain one of my best friends.

But things didn't work out. I was devastated when the courtship soured and she left. Back then we were all so young—she was only eighteen, and Kody and I were in our first year of marriage—so we may have mistaken a crush for love. Nevertheless, I felt personally betrayed. I had lost one of my closest friends, a woman I imagined would have been a perfect sister wife.

We managed to put our failed courtship behind us. Kody and I were still the fun-loving, goofy, and wildly romantic couple we'd always been, but we felt that adding a wife to our family was something we needed to accomplish sooner rather than later in order to make good on our commitment to the principle of plural marriage. This was a promise we made to each other when we married—as much as we loved each other and had a wonderful, stable relationship, we knew that plural marriage was our destiny.

I'm not sure when it became apparent to me that Janelle wanted to join our family. Of course, since she had once been married to my brother, I had known her for several years. We had a cordial relationship. Even after her divorce, I thought of her as a sister-in-law, and it never occurred to me that she would one day be a sister wife.

If Kody had feelings about Janelle that were anything other than platonic, he hadn't discussed them with me. I knew that he valued her intellect and her work ethic, and he had a deep respect for the way she conducted herself on an emotional level. I was surprised when Janelle approached Kody and asked to come into our family, but not unpleasantly so. After all, she was close to my family already, and she was one of the people Kody and I associated with on a fairly regular basis. So it didn't seem too far of a stretch to imagine her as a permanent fixture in our lives.

I have to admit, part of me was relieved that Kody and Janelle weren't a conventionally romantic couple. I didn't feel that Janelle's presence in our lives in any way threatened the love Kody and I shared. Their bond was intellectual, which made it easier for me to accept Janelle. If they had been one of those gushy, lovey-dovey couples, who melt at the sight of each other— if they had been the same kind of couple Kody and I were—I would have had a lot more trouble making peace with the idea of her as a sister wife.

I immediately saw that Kody and I would have one type of relationship—the passionate, romantic one we'd always had— while he and Janelle would have another, something more cerebral. This seemed both totally acceptable to me and easier to handle, as our first move into plural marriage.

After nearly three years of monogamous marriage, I was ready for a sister wife, or so I thought. I was happy for Kody that he'd found someone to satisfy his intellectual curiosity, and I was happy for Janelle to have chosen—and to have been chosen by—such a wonderful man after her failed relationship with my brother.

One thing that was difficult was the timing of Kody and Janelle's wedding—they planned it to take place on my birthday, thinking that it wouldn't be a big deal. Looking back, I realize a lot of my issues with their marriage were really because I thought they were being extremely insensitive. Birthdays are important to me! I felt like I was being completely overlooked, even when they offered to celebrate their future anniversaries on a different day. It floored me that my husband would think this was a good idea, but it baffled me even more to know that a woman who was wanting to join our family would even think for a minute to do it on the birthday of a future sister wife! Fortunately, Kody's mom got involved and persuaded them to move their wedding to the day *after* my birthday.

While I wished them all the happiness in the world, I was not as prepared as I believed myself to be. Kody and Janelle's courtship was so quick that when their wedding day arrived, I was struck by the realization that I was going to be sharing my husband. It was harder than I thought it would be. No matter how much you are committed to the principle of plural marriage, the first time the reality hits you, it's a total shock. For three years, Kody and I had been practically inseparable, and now there was going to be a new person in our midst. Permanently.

Their ceremony was simple but touching. I was happy for both of them, but I couldn't deny my own sadness, especially at the prospect of them leaving for their honeymoon. After all, Kody and I had barely been apart since we married. We spent every possible moment together. Now he was driving off for a week-long trip with another woman. No matter how hard I tried, it was difficult for me to come to terms with this.

Just before Kody left for his honeymoon with Janelle, he pulled me aside and handed me some money. "This is mad money," he said. "Go out and play. Spend it on whatever you want and enjoy yourself."

His gesture was so sweet and touching. My plan was to hole up in a hotel room and gorge on television viewing while I tried to make sense of my complicated feelings. Who was I, now that I wasn't "Meri and Kody"? When my mom and dad realized what I was intending to do, they insisted that I come stay at their house. I resisted at first. I couldn't imagine being around anyone and burdening them with my emotions. In the end my parents prevailed.

"This is a time when you need people around you," my mother explained. She knew, without my telling her, how much I was struggling inside.

My parents were completely right—instead of wallowing in a hotel by myself, I needed to be surrounded by family and friends. Despite my sadness, I managed to enjoy myself, which was really important because it made the week pass more quickly. Kody called me every day to check in and to tell me that he loved me.

When Janelle entered the family, Kody and I were still starry-eyed regarding the principle of plural marriage—and marriage in general—so we had no idea how to prepare for the emotional and domestic reality of our new situation. I guess we just assumed that after Kody and Janelle got married and went on their honeymoon, the three of us would live in one house as a big, happy family, and everything would go back to normal. Neither Kody nor I anticipated the need to change our behavior when Janelle came into the house. We didn't consider how he might have to balance the relationship he had with me with the one he was developing with Janelle. I never took the time to think about how I should open up my space—both physical and emotional—to accommodate a new wife.

I felt as if I was welcoming to Janelle, but I didn't realize at the time how different our personalities could be. We all moved into a new house about the time of Janelle's wedding, so I didn't feel like it was *my* house, but *our* house. When we were deciding who would get what bedroom, I offered Janelle the master bedroom, thinking it might be something special to have as a newlywed, while I took the small bedroom at the back of the house. I didn't realize then that Janelle wasn't the type to speak up for what she needed, so I don't know whether this was something that was important to her, or even appreciated. I assumed that Janelle would feel free to behave with Kody the same way I was with him, and I didn't realize I needed to change my behavior sometimes as well.

The biggest mistake we made when we married Janelle was us all moving into a house together and not giving Janelle and me the space we needed to develop and nurture our own relationships with Kody. Having us all in the same house brought Janelle face-to-face on a daily basis with the romantic relationship Kody and I had. We were too naive to hide our affection for each other from Janelle, and I'm afraid to say that she was confronted by it regularly, which I'm sure was both painful and awkward. At times, Kody and I would hold hands or hug each other in front of Janelle, leaving her in what was probably a very uncomfortable situation.

Although Janelle is by no means as physically affectionate a person as I am, it was not healthy or fair for her to see the affection I shared with Kody. I'm sure this led to hard feelings toward me. Living together from the start ultimately shortchanged the three relationships we were trying to develop and maintain.

Another reason that Kody and Janelle had difficulties laying the foundation for their marriage during that first year was that they were essentially living under a veil of secrecy. Kody was simply unable to acknowledge Janelle as his wife outside of our church community.

We were very quiet and private when it came to our family life, which I'm sure didn't help Janelle feel secure in her position in the family. When we went out together somewhere other than church associations, we always introduced Janelle as Kody's sister. I remember on more than one occasion that Kody, Janelle, and I had a conversation about how to explain who Janelle was. Kody and I already lived and worked in the small community in Wyoming when Janelle joined the family, so it was Janelle whom we felt we needed to explain. Looking back, I realize it wasn't fair to Kody and Janelle's relationship to refer to her as his sister.

Since Janelle's mom was married to Kody's dad, it seemed to be a reasonable explanation, and it always seemed as if Janelle was okay with this reference. I always felt a bit uncomfortable referring to her this way, but she and Kody seemed to be okay with it, so I played along. I believe it did a major disservice to Kody and Janelle's marriage.

After Kody married Janelle, I went through a sort of separation anxiety. I missed the privacy of our old situation—the luxury of making a romantic dinner for just Kody and myself whenever I wanted, or renting a good movie and curling up on the couch together. These are things you simply can't do when another wife enters the picture and is living in the same house. It can be perceived as preferential treatment and that is just not okay in a plural marriage. This anxiety put a strain on Kody's and my relationship and made me at times act unfairly to both him and Janelle.

I have to admit that I didn't always handle the stress of the new situation as I should have. I didn't know how to hold back or temper my opinions. I am a very direct person, and when I have a strong opinion about something, I can be a little bit harsh. Since I see things in black and white, I have a bad habit of phrasing things in a way that can come across as aggressive. Janelle, on the other hand, is quite nonconfrontational and seems to have a hard time being honest with herself, or with others, about her feelings. I'd tell Janelle that "this is how it needs to be," and didn't realize I was offering her no space to voice her own concerns. I didn't intend to be mean, I wasn't even aware that I was coming across that way. I was being honest with my thoughts and feelings and just assumed she would do the same.

I remember having conversations with her many times concerning everything—from how the house should be decorated to how the finances should be handled. I would tell her how I thought the situation should be taken care of, and because I had that type of personality, I just assumed she would voice her opinion as well. When I would find out later, through Kody, that there was an issue or disagreement, I was so upset that she didn't tell me her thoughts or opinions while we were having the discussion. I felt as if she was lying to me, and I felt betrayed by this. I thought we were in this marriage together to have a close, if not completely open, relationship, and didn't understand why she wouldn't communicate honestly with me, when that's what I was trying to do with her. I hadn't yet learned how to be softer in the delivery of my words and not so overbearing.

Naturally, the tentative friendship I had with Janelle deteriorated even more in the months following her marriage to Kody. I had hoped that with her in the family, we would be able to work on improving our relationship. I wanted, and almost expected, to have a special sister wife bond with Janelle. I realized early on, however, that wouldn't be the case. Janelle seemed very reserved toward me, as far as becoming close friends. I felt that I had to accept that we wouldn't have the close sister wife relationship that I had always hoped for. To make things worse, Kody had taken a job setting up new accounts for Schwan's Frozen Foods, which required him to be on the road for long stretches of time. This left Janelle and me at home with our growing list of complaints against each other. Since Kody was new to the principle and the practice of plural marriage, he had no idea how to negotiate between the two of us. I know he was aware of the tension between us, and did his best to deal with it, but we all were going to have to sort out our new roles, and learn how to live together and love one another.

During the early years of our plural family, there were many emotions rolling around among all of us—mostly, I feel safe to say, between Janelle and me. In living plural marriage, you definitely have to go through a huge learning curve. Janelle and I had a lot of rough times in those early years. We both did and said things to each other that I'm sure we would like to forget. There is a lot of past history, things that I won't talk about in specifics in public out of my respect for Janelle, and my desire to protect her. Even now, we still struggle with the residue of those early years. I truly hope that Janelle and I can work through some of those haunting issues of the past, so they will stop recurring in our lives. Someday, when we're both ready, I hope it will happen.

While Janelle, through no fault of her own, brought a level of tension to the house, she also brought her own strengths to the marriage. Kody was busy with his job at Schwan's while I was engaged in my own job hunt. Janelle urged me to apply for the job as an engraver at a trophy company, a job I would hold for ten years. Eventually, moments like that would help us appreciate what our relationship could be.

The most difficult emotional battle I would face during the first year after Janelle joined our family was when she got pregnant. Kody and I had been married for three years and, naturally, we'd been trying to conceive. But we'd had no success. So when Janelle conceived before I did, I was pretty devastated, even though deep down, I had expected it.

I could immediately see how thrilled Kody was by Janelle's news. While I tried to be as happy as possible about the first child coming into the Brown family, I felt betrayed by my own body. It had let me down and made me feel like both a disappointment and a failure. I couldn't figure out what was wrong with me, so I turned inward and started to withdraw from Kody and Janelle.

At the time of Janelle's pregnancy with her first child, Logan, Kody decided to pursue a courtship with Christine. We had all become friends soon after Kody and I got married. Somehow, in the back of my mind, this courtship had always seemed inevitable.

Kody's courtship with Christine was much more difficult for

me than his with Janelle had been. I never felt that Janelle threatened the overall happiness Kody and I shared. Kody and Janelle were friends, very close friends. I knew Kody loved Janelle, but it was in a totally different way than he loved me. Around her, he never behaved in the silly, romantic way he did with me. I found this reassuring. When Janelle came into our family, the day-to-day nature of my marriage with Kody changed, but our relationship stayed the same. Despite having added a second wife to our lives, I never felt that Kody loved me any less than the day we were married.

With Christine, however, things were different. Christine was cute and energetic. She was young and girly, and quite flirtatious. I had always suspected that Kody was more than a little smitten with her—and when they began to court, I could immediately sense that Kody was not just smitten but in love. The two of them glowed around each other. They had fun with each other and loved to goof off together. Where Kody and Janelle's courtship had been less outwardly romantic, this new relationship was grounded in an undeniable emotional attraction.

When Kody proposed to Christine, I suddenly felt as if I were less important to him than I had been before. I felt threatened by their relationship and the friendship they'd built over the first three years of my marriage to Kody. Although she was our mutual friend, I always knew that Kody was somewhat taken with Christine. Kody seemed so much more engaged with Christine than he had been with Janelle. I think that he had learned from the experience of bringing Janelle into the family how he needed to behave with Christine—how much more expressive and responsive he had to be to her needs and wants. He had gained knowledge from his relationship with Janelle and seemed much wiser when it came to courting Christine. He also seemed more devoted to the cause—at least that's how it appeared to me. It cemented my feelings of inadequacy in our relationship when Kody called me only once while he and Christine were away on their honeymoon.

When Christine came into our family, she chose to live in a different house rather than squeeze into the same house that Janelle and I shared. She wanted her own experience with Kody before joining the "family" experience, so she moved into a small cottage nearby. Even though this meant Kody would be spending several nights a week out of our house, it seemed like a healthier and more reasonable choice for everyone.

Although I had a hard time with Kody and Christine's courtship, I was surprised by how easily I became friends with Christine. Of course, this didn't happen overnight, but her fun and outgoing personality livened up the mood in our household. Eventually, Christine and I discovered that we shared the same predilection for silliness and we almost always managed to embarrass Janelle with our antics.

Although Christine and I had a much easier relationship than I had with Janelle, I couldn't help my disappointment when she, too, became pregnant. Nearly five years into my marriage with Kody, I was beginning to worry that I'd never have a baby.

When Christine was four months pregnant with her first child, Kody started urging me to take a pregnancy test. My period was a little late, but that was nothing out of the ordinary for me. Still, he wouldn't let the subject drop. Eventually, I agreed and took the test. I absolutely could not believe it when the little stripe on the stick told me I was pregnant. I was certain the test had made a mistake. But it hadn't. I could barely contain my joy!

The next morning, Janelle and I drove to Christine's house to pick up her and Kody for church. I was struggling to hide my excitement. I couldn't wait to share my news with Kody, but I had to. I wanted to tell him about our baby privately, not blurt it out in front of everyone in the car.

Sometime in the middle of church, Kody remembered the

pregnancy test. He got my attention and shot a knowing glance down at my stomach. At first I tried to ignore him. But he kept looking at my belly. Finally, I just nodded. The most enormous smile I'd ever seen burst onto Kody's face, and his eyes welled up with tears of joy.

Kody and I were beside ourselves with happiness. The very thing we'd been hoping for since we got married had finally happened. We were going to have our first child.

The only thing that tempered my joy a little was knowing that Christine was going to have a hard time with my pregnancy. She was new in the family and four months pregnant with her first child, and now here I was pregnant after a five-year struggle. I was carrying a miracle baby. I was afraid that a lot of the focus would shift from her to me. While I didn't blame her for being slightly resentful that I stole her thunder, I tried not to dwell on it. I was so excited and happy that I'd finally gotten what I'd always wanted.

After Mariah was born, I was certain that I was going to have more children. My entire life I'd always wanted eight kids. In fact, when Kody and I started dating, this was something we talked about on a regular basis. But once I had Mariah, my body didn't want to give me any more children. Kody and I tried everything to help me conceive, from medical doctors to holistic healers, but nothing worked. The most difficult thing for me was knowing that the fertility problem lay with me, not with Kody. Since Janelle and Christine got pregnant so often and so easily, it was clear that Kody had no problem fathering children. I struggled to come to terms with the fact that I was somehow defective.

Kody never once made me feel bad for the fact that I wasn't able to get pregnant again. Yet I sometimes couldn't help but feel that my sister wives used their pregnancies to validate their marriages to Kody in a way I couldn't. I know they never intentionally flaunted their fertility, but because I struggled so much with my infertility issues, I often wondered what place I had in the family.

When Mariah was twelve years old, I'd pretty much given up all hope of having another child. Then, completely out of the blue, I got pregnant again. My joy, however, was short-lived, and I lost the baby after only a couple of months. I was devastated. My body simply didn't want to have any more children. I was blessed with one and I would have to be content with that. There would be no more babies in my future.

During the twelve years between Mariah's birth and my second unsuccessful pregnancy, our family went through a lot of growing pains. I know that Janelle struggled to find her path in our midst and was always on the lookout for a way to assert her own identity in such a large family with three wives and twelve children. We had to learn to work together and to make decisions in a way that put our family first.

The root of many of our problems stemmed from two issues—our living situation and Kody's job. Kody was often employed in positions that required him to travel a lot, which would essentially leave the three wives behind, functioning as single mothers. During a period when he was on the road a lot, Janelle moved into her own house. Although she and I had been struggling under one roof for nearly ten years, the separation of our children was difficult.

For the most part, we hid our lifestyle from the public. Yet there were people who were aware that we were a polygamous family. Some of these people would refer to "Kody and his families." This always rubbed me the wrong way. Despite our differences, we were one big family who happened to be divided into three different houses. Our separation was causing an identity crisis. How can you be one unit if you are living apart? How can Kody be the best dad possible if he isn't present for all of his children all of the time?

During this time, Janelle and I both had jobs while Christine took care of the majority of day care and homeschooling. Eventually, Kody found a job in Utah that didn't require any travel. This meant that he would be present in our children's lives on a much more regular basis.

While this was a major and important development in our lives, what really changed our situation and brought us together as a family was when we found a house in which our entire family could live together under one roof. The house had formerly belonged to a polygamous family. It was a large home, divided into three separate yet attached apartments—one for each wife. This was the perfect solution to many of our struggles. It joined us into one, unshakable family. The big house allowed us to forge and cement our identity as a family.

This house allowed Kody to be home with his kids every night. He would be able to see all his children equally. In other words, even if Kody was to be at my house on a particular night, he would still be able to see Janelle's and Christine's kids—tuck them in and do all the fatherly things that would have been impossible for him if we'd still been living in separate houses.

Around this time, I really started coming to terms with the fact that there were no more biological kids in my future. However, now that we were living in one house, I was able to come to a deeper appreciation of the blessings that plural marriage has provided me. While I cannot have any more children of my own, I have been able, through my sister wives, to give Mariah many brothers and sisters. She has siblings her age—peers with whom she can share all the experiences of growing up—as well as siblings who are younger and look up to her. If I hadn't chosen polygamy—if I hadn't been called to it and listened to that call—

I would never have achieved the large family I'd always dreamed of having. Plural marriage has blessed me with what my body denied me.

I have a wonderful relationship with all the kids in our family. Naturally, with so many children, I'm closer to some than to others. It's hard to describe my relationship to all the children who are not biologically mine. I have been an essential part of their upbringing, in the same way that Janelle and Christine have been a part of Mariah's. I may not be their biological mother, but I am a mother to them.

Since I have more time on my hands and since my living area is always quite a bit more peaceful than the others, I'm the mom the kids come to when they want a little quiet time away from their siblings. They call it "Meri Time." It's a wonderful feeling knowing there is a huge pack of children who love me and want to hang out and have fun with me.

When we moved into the big house in Utah, the one featured on the first season of *Sister Wives,* it was time to start working through a lot of my difficulties with Janelle. We are both incredibly devoted to our family and our faith, and despite our differences, we are committed to creating the best, safest, and warmest environment for our kids.

Often, people ask me if I'd be friends with my sister wives if they weren't married to my husband. This is a difficult question, but goes a long way to understanding the nature of sister wives. Janelle and I are very different people; we see the world in opposite ways and handle situations in entirely different manners. I'm sure if we weren't married to Kody, our friendship wouldn't have gone past basic cordiality. But since we share a husband, a lot of our differences are brought out into the open and confrontation is impossible to avoid.

The nature of our singular relationship has forced us to confront those differences and examine the way we treat each other.

While it's true that Janelle and I each chose to marry Kody, we weren't truly aware of the relationship and struggles that lay ahead. Because of our commitment to our family, we have to find a path down which we can travel together.

One of the benefits of polygamy is that as you grow in the religion, you are forced to examine yourself and your treatment of others, especially your sister wives, with whom you often have complicated relationships. Polygamists and polygamous families are often works in progress. Janelle and I have never had a close relationship—we don't gossip on the phone or grab lunch in our free time. I don't think that we will ever sit down and tell each other our deep, dark secrets. But we are family, and for that reason we love each other.

We've worked hard to develop a good and functional relationship because we've come to understand that this is what is best for the family, and when it comes to family, we share the same values. We are not just good with each other's kids, we absolutely love each one of them. We are devoted to our lifestyle and to the hard work we'd discovered it takes to make it work. We've learned that there will always be bumps in the road, but the work is certainly worth it.

On February 6, 2006, my younger sister Teresa passed away after an eleven-month battle with colon cancer. This was an unbelievably difficult experience for me, but it forced me to confront my own mortality. It made me realize that should something happen to me, there would be two (and now three) women in Mariah's life who would raise her in precisely the way I would have wished. She would be loved and cared for by a stable and miraculous family. For me, there could be no greater blessing.

Despite the fact that our living situation and Kody's work situation stabilized, I still felt the need to carve out my own space in the boisterous and often chaotic Brown family. Since I only have one child, I often felt slighted in family decisions. Although

I voiced my opinions perhaps a little too aggressively, I still felt as if I wasn't being taken into consideration.

It's easy to lose yourself in a big family. When we lived in Wyoming when the older kids were young, Christine and I homeschooled them and handled the household upkeep. While Janelle was working full-time, Christine and I each worked part-time so that at least one of us moms could be home with the kids all the time. When we moved back to Utah when Mariah was ten, I started working immediately, while Christine took on the duty of the homemaker mom. I realized that while nothing trumps my commitment to the family, it's important to have things that I can do myself and for myself.

Over time, my insecurity about having only one child grew. As Mariah got older and was more independent, I began to wonder how important I was to the everyday goings-on of our family. I began to wonder if it would even matter if I wasn't around. I never really considered leaving, but was anxious about my place and function in our daily lives. I felt insignificant, to myself and definitely to Janelle and Christine. To me, it didn't seem as if they saw any point to my being in the family. I knew that I would have to make some changes if I were to regain my own identity and happiness.

I had always wanted to go to college, but since Kody and I married so young, I didn't give myself this chance. However, I didn't want to start school unless I had a clear idea of what I wanted to do. My family often jokes about my sudden, intuitive ideas they call "popcorn thoughts"—ideas that pop into my head from out of nowhere. One morning as I was getting ready for work, I had one of these so-called popcorn thoughts. I had the notion that I was going to work with at-risk youth. It completely surprised me, and I tried to push the thought aside, but as the days and weeks passed, and the thought kept nagging at me, I figured I needed to pay attention to it.

Finally, I told Kody about it. At first I don't think he understood how serious I was about it, and therefore he didn't seem very supportive of me. However, the idea didn't disappear. I began to realize that I needed an outlet outside of the family. I really wanted to do something for myself, as well as something that would help others. I think that the fact that I had only one child, which made me feel at times less significant than my sister wives, really propelled me to search for something that would fulfill me.

When I enrolled at Utah Valley University and took classes in counseling, Kody realized how committed I was to this new career. Both he and my sister wives were very encouraging—everyone helped out as I balanced the demands of my new course load against those of my job and family. Eventually, I got a job working with the residential staff at a treatment center for troubled teens. I was incredibly satisfied with my job. I was eager to get my degree and start working as a counselor myself.

I think that due to the space that each of us wives had for ourselves, coupled with how easy it was to come together as a large family unit in our new home, things had stabilized in our household. We had all become used to one another's quirks and differences. We all had a maturity about us, because of our age and the length of time we had been together as a family raising our kids. Not all of the relationships in the house were fully functional, but we had learned how to put aside minor disagreements for the greater good. I think the fact that Janelle and I were both happy in our professions, and Christine seemed to be doing a great job at home, really added to the general happy attitude in the home.

After sixteen years—and thirteen kids!—Kody, Janelle, Christine, and I had figured out who we were as a family and how to make things work. We were a well-oiled unit and we could see this reflected in our children's happiness. Although the Brown family was functioning, my relationship with Kody was floundering. After nearly twenty years of marriage, issues that we had left to simmer had begun to boil over.

Around the time that Kody and I were suffering through this low point in our marriage, we decided to take a drive together. It was a particularly good day for us, as we had been working on improving our relationship and the communication between us. We were passing by our friend Reba's house and we stopped to say hello. A young woman, Reba's cousin, was outside loading her children into a van in order to drive back home to southern Utah. We started chatting. I felt an immediate connection to her. After we drove away, I was instantly struck by one of my "popcorn thoughts": *This woman is someone who will be in our lives.* Of course, that woman was Robyn.

I shared my thoughts with Kody that night, which was the first step on the path of welcoming her into our family. Until that time, I wasn't sure if Kody would ever marry again. If he did, I would have never imagined my being so closely involved from the start.

We soon discovered that Robyn was divorced but believed in the principle of plural marriage. Kody and I began to talk about her between ourselves. It didn't seem necessary to bring up the subject of Robyn to the rest of the family until it was more apparent that there might be a potential for courtship—so she became a little connection that Kody and I shared, a sweet special bond in a time of turmoil between us.

Since things were rocky between Kody and me, it was a little unusual to consider bringing a new wife into the picture, especially given that I never, ever thought that Robyn would solve my problems with Kody. I just felt drawn to her in a way that satisfied me. I wanted her as a friend and I had a clear vision of her in our lives. Janelle and Christine had not yet met her, so this little relationship between Kody, Robyn, and me felt special.

At first, the three of us had a wonderful friendship. But when the time came for Robyn to start exploring her relationship with Kody on a deeper and more personal level, things became difficult for me. I had been instrumental in bringing Robyn and Kody together and now I wasn't needed anymore. Since Robyn lived so far away, Kody had to spend much more time away from the house in order to court her. At first, he'd take a wife and a couple of kids with him on these trips, as the whole family would need to get to know Robyn and her children. Eventually, it was better for him to not include the wives, as he and Robyn deserved and needed time alone to build their own relationship. Robyn's presence transformed from something that filled me with joy to something that made me extremely lonely, as well as feeling the love that Kody and I shared was once again being threatened.

Kody and Robyn started courting at the absolute low point of my marriage. Our twenty-year anniversary was fast approaching and I was learning that so much time together will either make you or break you. Kody and I have very different ways of communicating. He is happy to just stop talking about the issue and move on, never discussing it, and considering it dealt with, while I really need to discuss it and achieve some kind of closure on the subject. Because of our different communication styles, Kody and I found it easier to ignore our problems instead of addressing them. Things that might have been solved quickly suddenly ballooned. Over a twenty-year marriage, with all the pressures of other wives and other kids, this led to a significant amount of misunderstanding and strife between us.

When Kody and Robyn began courting, I realized that the two of us needed to take steps to repair our own relationship. Because I felt insignificant and insecure in my relationship with Kody, I struggled with all the time that he needed to spend with Robyn and her kids in southern Utah. Again, I turned inward and began to wonder what benefit I was to this family. Kody and I were hanging by a thread and he was off courting someone else. Even though courting Robyn had been partly my idea, the reality of the situation was very difficult for me.

I liked Robyn, and I felt a connection to her, and I wanted Kody to court her, but when it came down to it and I was actually dealing with those emotions on top of the emotions I was already having in my struggling relationship with Kody, it became very difficult to deny the hurt.

Kody and I had fallen into a vicious cycle with each other, dealing with hurt, anger, rejection, and sadness. It got to the point where we didn't really enjoy being around each other, and when we were together, we could barely say anything without setting the other off. We talked little, and enjoyed each other's company even less. I felt as if Kody was shutting me out of his life almost completely. Eventually, we had to look at each other deep and hard and decide what we really wanted. How committed were we, and were we willing to fight for each other, and get back what we once had?

Kody and I decided together that we needed to see a marriage counselor. We needed to feel solid in our relationship as he moved on with his courtship with Robyn. I know Robyn was also anxious for us to mend our marriage before she came into our family. It took a long time, and a lot of hard sessions with us being absolutely open and honest with each other. It was probably one of the hardest things I have ever done in my life. It was also the best thing I have ever done. This counselor helped us work through our problems and uncover a common language with which to communicate. Kody learned to be more patient with me when I brought my problems to him. He learned to let me talk them out. I was able to confront my anger and started to understand that sometimes my aggressive attitude made it difficult for Kody to listen to me. It took a lot of hard work, but now Kody and I are at our absolute best. We are still (or again) very much in love. It is a wonderful thing knowing that Kody is absolutely my soul mate.

Our counselor had previously worked with plural families and was open and understanding about the joys and difficulties of our lifestyle. Meeting with this marriage counselor only strengthened my commitment to getting my own license so that I could use my experience in a polygamous family to help other polygamists who are struggling with themselves, their spouses, or their sister wives.

When she decided to join our family, Robyn took an active role in trying to forge a good relationship with me. She was patient with me and took the time to listen to me when I was struggling with my feelings and emotions. She began to see the same counselor that Kody and I did. Sometimes we did counseling as a group of three and sometimes Robyn and I did our own "couples counseling" in order to work through our issues before they were allowed to fester and blow up into large-scale disagreements and struggles.

The relationship between Kody and Robyn was new and exciting, and I could see how happy they were together. Since Kody and I had been married for so long, and our relationship was in a different stage—added to the fact that we were in a really tough spot—it was easy for me to put the blame on Robyn. In my head, I was sure that Kody wouldn't be treating me so unfairly if it wasn't for her presence in our lives. Kody was my husband, so I couldn't blame him, and surely *I* couldn't be at fault, so in my mind, the obvious answer was Robyn. I couldn't have been more wrong.

Robyn and I needed to figure out how to have a healthy friendship outside of our marriages to Kody, and I had to learn not to blame Robyn for my own struggles with Kody. I had to begin looking inward and admit my own shortcomings so I could improve myself. I needed to learn how to be open to seeing myself how I truly was appearing to people, and open to allowing Robyn into my world. My relationships with Janelle and Christine were longtime relationships, and we were comfortable where we were, but I wasn't completely happy with either of them. Janelle and I have learned how to function well together. We don't have an extremely close relationship, but it's good. Christine and I know how to goof off and have fun together. Our relationship is good on a surface level, but has absolutely no depth to it. When I first met Robyn, I knew there was a special closeness waiting for us, but I needed to learn how to be available and safe for her to want to let me in. If I hadn't been able to examine myself and be willing to begin my journey of improving myself, I wouldn't have found the sweet, close, sister wife bond that I had always hoped for. Robyn and I have arrived at such a wonderful place, which is a testament to me of what a beautiful principle our family has engaged in. Sometimes, when it's Kody's night at my house, Robyn and her kids will spend the evening with us, visiting or watching TV, or laughing at her little girls as they sing karaoke. I've never had to ask her to give Kody and me space; she is so sensitive and aware of what I need that she's always a step ahead. We have learned to respect each other's marriages and, out of this, our own friendship has grown beyond strong.

Of course, there can always be the little, silly struggles I have with my sister wives. We are all figuring out a way to interact with Kody when the five of us are together in public or private. We are all uncomfortable with him being affectionate with another sister wife in front of us. When we're all together at one wife's house, and the family get-together has ended, we've learned that we need to allow Kody a little time and space with each wife as she leaves to go home with her children. It would be uncomfortable for all of us to be standing there waiting to leave as he went down the line kissing each of us good night!

I want more privacy than that, and I think each wife deserves the same thing. There's an emotional intimacy that Kody has with each of his wives that is private and personal to each of us, and we need to allow one another the time and space to embrace it. Some might think that after being married for so long, it wouldn't bother us to see Kody kissing or hugging or saying "I love you" to someone else. It is really more a matter of respecting one another's space and relationship than it is of jealousy.

It's not a hard-and-fast rule, but I believe that one of the key factors in being a good sister wife is having the ability to see the needs of another sister wife and considering her needs more important than your own. I have been on both the giving and receiving end, and not only does it help build my relationship with Kody, but it strengthens my relationships with all my sister wives. Also, it is very important to allow Kody and a wife to have their own relationship, not having to be bothered with outside concerns. We have a lot of family time that involves all of us, but when it's time for Kody and a wife to have their own time, I make it a habit to not call him unless it's something extremely important. Even at that, I will usually just text him, and allow him to respond when it's convenient for him. For me, it's as simple as "do unto others. . . ." I wouldn't want my time with Kody to be interrupted unnecessarily, so I make a point of respecting my sister wives' time with him equally.

One of the benefits of plural marriage is that you are forced to confront your own weakness of character and work on being the best wife, sister, and mother you can be. I'm confident that I would not be the person I am today if I had chosen a monogamous marriage.

When Robyn married Kody, she thanked Janelle, Christine, and me for training him to be the guy he is now. Like myself, Kody is so much more emotionally mature than he was when we married. But Robyn is not the sole beneficiary of this growth.

After twenty-two years, Kody and I are better than ever. We share a deep and passionate love, and finally understand each other's love language.

When we moved to Las Vegas, we soon discovered that we weren't going to be able to find a house both large enough for the family and with the specific qualities we needed. We decided instead on four separate homes so each wife and her children would have the space they needed to nurture their individual relationships with Kody, while at the same time choosing homes close enough together that we could still function as a family. While I wish for Mariah's sake that she could be closer to her siblings, I've really learned to love my space. Some days, I want the chaos of the whole family, and some nights, when Kody isn't around, I want to be able to sit up and watch TV, read a book, or work on a project as late as I want without disturbing anybody. Essentially, I have the best of both worlds.

Since we moved to Las Vegas, and are in separate homes with an even busier schedule than we once had, I don't always see Kody every day. In fact, recently we went five full days without seeing each other! With the growth that our relationship has had in the past couple of years, I often think of the saying, "Absence makes the heart grow fonder." When I do see Kody, it always feels new and refreshing. We've missed each other and we are delighted to see each other.

When we go to family reunions and I see my family members who are monogamists, I often wonder, "How can you have your husband around all the time? When do you have time for yourself?" I can't imagine their lifestyle. But then again, they can't understand mine either. I would never trade my experience with sister wives and the wonderfully large and dynamic family we share for the simplicity of monogamy. I wouldn't trade it for anything in the world.

Chapter Six

JANELLE

I was enchanted with the idea of polygamy when I married Kody. I was in love with my new faith, with the possibilities of love, family, and sisterhood it offered. I imagined that my new sister wife, Meri, would immediately become my best friend. I believed that Kody would have no trouble navigating between us. I was so taken with the storybook notion of happily ever after that I was completely unprepared for the reality that awaited me.

Immediately after moving in with Meri and Kody, I began to lose my sense of self. While I never once doubted that I'd made the right decisions in choosing both Kody and my new faith, I struggled to find my way in my new life and lifestyle.

When I was young, I lacked self-esteem. I struggled with body image and didn't excel in any particular area in school. As I grew up and graduated from high school, I slowly started to find my way in the world. I realized what was important to me and what I valued. I discovered that I enjoyed working. I knew that in addition to having children, having a career would be one of the things that would matter most to me and bring me a sense of security and happiness.

I have always been happiest when I've devoted myself to my work. Although I wasn't sure what career path to follow—human resources, accounting, bookkeeping—I was determined to advance myself in the workplace. Especially when my first marriage failed, working gave me inner strength and confidence.

After Kody and I returned from our honeymoon, I moved into the guest bedroom of his and Meri's house. In no time, I came to feel like a guest who had overstayed her welcome. I felt like I'd barged not just into their house but into their marriage. Meri and I went from cordial to frosty overnight. We sniped at each other over the smallest things. When she was younger, Meri had quite an overbearing personality.

It was clear I was unable to do anything right—or rather, in a way that suited Meri. I folded Kody's clothes incorrectly. I bought the wrong dish soap and put away the dishes in the wrong places. I learned never, ever to fold Meri's laundry for her, but to leave it in the dryer long after the buzzer signaled that it was done. She made it clear I was disrupting her household.

I was raised in a family that believed in keeping the waters smooth—I'm a pleaser. I was raised to be nonconfrontational. So I caved to Meri on all fronts. Many, many times I wanted to tell her off, give her a piece of my mind, but I just buttoned my lip and did things her way as best as I could.

I never felt as if the house was mine in any way. I kept to my bedroom as much as possible. We were all so young then and new to this principle in both theory and practice. I know now that our experience is by no means unusual for young plural families and that the first year of living the principle is far and away the most difficult. Many couples do not press past this year. But divorce was never a question for us. We were committed to the lifestyle, as difficult and stressful as it may have been.

Our main problem was that we all lived under one roof, which never allowed me sufficient alone time with Kody. Kody didn't know how to behave as my husband in Meri's house. When we watched a movie together at night, Kody and Meri would sit together on the couch while I felt left out in the cold. So I learned to separate myself.

I began to physically distance myself as much as I could in our very small three-bedroom mobile home. I didn't spend much time in the common areas, instead setting up my bedroom as my living space. Kody was gone at his sales job from six thirty in the morning until ten thirty at night, six days a week, which made it even more uncomfortable. I would spend time at work, go out to spend time at the family ranch, and then come home and go straight to my room.

I continued to pursue my study of Native American arts and crafts and wild plant herbology, both of which were easier to undertake in the rural environment of the family ranch. My mother and Kody's father lived only a half hour away, so I spent as much time as I could up there. I threw myself into life on the ranch, helping out as much as I could. Working outdoors helped me create an identity for myself outside of the family that I had just joined. It allowed me to clear my head and regain some sense of self.

Meri and I were stuck at home with our disagreements far too often in the first years after I joined the family. We rarely spoke to each other, but we tolerated each other. We were like roommates who didn't get along but managed to live together all the same. This was not the celestial plural marriage I'd imagined. It was uncomfortable and disheartening.

Often Kody would take Meri with him when he worked out of state, which made me very resentful of her. I couldn't just take off from work, as she seemed to be able to. But when Meri didn't work, she didn't get paid—I thought it was extremely flaky to blow off work for fun like that, especially when we were so broke. Some of the family clucked their tongues when they saw

Kody and Meri drive off on Sunday night after dinner at the ranch, leaving me to go home alone to our house in Powell.

I was left at home in an unfamiliar small town in Wyoming, far away from most of the people I knew. This was the first time in my life I'd lived anywhere without many relatives or friends nearby. It was a terribly bleak time for me.

My mother, of course, lived on the ranch where I spent a lot of time. She was the only person I could rely on during this difficult phase. While we were able to commiserate a decent amount, she was also going through her own adjustment period. Like me, she was new to polygamy and didn't have all, or even any, of the answers about how things should be and how they should work.

Adjusting to any marriage, let alone a plural one, is an incredibly individual experience, and it is all-encompassing. Your entire worldview and your entire cultural, personal, and religious awareness goes through a radical upheaval. You barely have time to worry about what's going on in the outside world. I found that I had to do so much work readjusting my own parameters and shifting my own perspectives that I didn't think too much about my mother's parallel experiences. While I was aware that my mother was involved in many of the same personal and emotional struggles as I was, we didn't discuss them often. We supported each other and were available to each other, but we never explored the depths of our conversion together. We were both too wrapped up in our own transitions to examine these things as a team.

Even though my mother and I never discussed our initial experiences with polygamy with one another, it was comforting to have her within driving distance. When I moved to Powell from Utah to marry Kody, I hadn't simply left all of my friends and family behind, but I'd also alienated many of them by accepting polygamy.

My sister and her husband tried to intervene and pull me back into the LDS faith. Some of my other family members even went so far as to stage a small-scale intervention to reconvert me, or as they saw it, save me. When I was eight months pregnant with Logan, Kody, Christine, and I visited Salt Lake. I took the opportunity to see some of my relatives. Kody and Christine had dropped me off at my relatives' house, so I was without a car until they returned. I guess my family decided to take advantage of the fact that I was a captive audience until Kody got back. They cornered me in the living room and began hurling Mormon scripture at me. They told me that what I was doing by living with Kody (they didn't recognize our marriage) was wrong. They said that I was giving up my blessings. I was furious and hurt. Eventually, I disengaged myself from them and told them they could "go hang it in their ears." I ran upstairs and waited for Kody and Christine to return.

Many of my other relatives, such as my maternal grandfather, never forgave me and did not speak to me again. Over time, I've rebuilt many of these relationships, but those first years when I was new to the principle, losing my family really hurt. At least, I still had my mother for support. She was by my side at our family gatherings, which made me feel as if I was not entirely shunned.

Normally, I would have turned to my career as an outlet to bolster my self-confidence. But when I married Kody, I'd been forced to quit my stable job in Utah and move to Wyoming— a small town with few employment opportunities. While I did manage to find a job, I felt that I had wandered far off course from my career goals.

About six months after marrying Kody, I discovered that I was pregnant. Naturally, I was thrilled. I had something of my own, something that would, at least in part, make me feel as if I were an important member of the Brown family. Even though I hadn't managed to figure out who I was and how I fit into the family I had joined, I was proud to be bringing the first child into our world.

I knew that it would be uncomfortable telling Meri that I was pregnant. She had been unable to conceive after three years of marriage. However, I have to say that I didn't care how she felt about my news. If it upset her, so be it. Things were incredibly tough in our relationship, so her feelings were of little importance to me at that moment.

Kody, of course, was beyond excited at the thought of becoming a father. But our happiness did little to smooth over the tensions in the household. During my pregnancy, relations between Meri and me reached an all-time low. I was physically exhausted and sick, which weakened my ability to put up with Meri's snide remarks and jabs. While she never overtly made me feel unwelcome in the house, I rarely ventured out into the rest of the home. I felt completely disenfranchised, even though I was carrying Kody's child.

Just before one of those trips when I was being left behind once more, my pregnancy hormones were making me feel especially vulnerable. Kody had taken a new job logging on a mountain, and I was upset to learn that he was again taking Meri with him. Meri took advantage of the situation to be exceptionally brutal. One of my friends and I had experimented with my makeup. As I was crying that I was being left behind, Meri began to ridicule the makeup I was wearing. This was the final straw after all the passive-aggressive behavior and snide remarks I had been dealing with for so many months. I completely lost it. I felt as if I was on the verge of a complete nervous breakdown. Kody was on his way out the door when I stopped him. There were tears running down my face.

"I just need to know that you love me," I said.

A strange expression spread across Kody's face. I felt as if he was going to laugh, not out of cruelty, but out of relief.

"Of course I love you," he said.

"That's all I needed to hear," I told him.

"That's it?" Kody said. "That's all I needed to say?"

I managed to nod through my tears. The smallest things make the greatest difference. But we were all so young and we had taken on so much. Kody had a lot of learning to do. He was still a naive twenty-five-year-old. His father, his mother, Meri's parents, and my mom were giving him advice from all sides. But ultimately, Kody would have to listen to himself and to his wives to achieve his own emotional maturity and understanding.

Right before I gave birth to Logan, Kody began courting and then married Christine. I was so committed to the principle that it didn't occur to me to be jealous. In fact, I was really excited at the prospect of having a wife in the family besides Meri and me. I suspected that Christine's arrival would take a lot of Meri's focus off me—get me out of the line of fire, if you will.

During their brief courtship, I was heavily pregnant, so I didn't have a lot of time or energy to worry about a new sister wife. I didn't know Christine as well as Meri did, but she seemed nice and sweet—if a little naive. It was clear to me that Christine didn't just want a relationship with Kody, she wanted to join our family, which made me happy. It seemed like she would be a good fit with us. I expected we would be better friends than Meri and I were, and I looked forward to that.

Christine joined the family only a few months before Logan was born. She and I had our differences, but nothing serious. At first, Christine came across as something of a little princess. I was baffled by the fact that Christine didn't believe that she needed to work in order to contribute to the family. (It's funny to say these things now, because over the years, Christine has morphed into the cornerstone of our household's stability and has worked tirelessly for everyone.) Back then, however, she had little experience living apart from her parents, and was clueless about many practical things. Initially, this grated on me.

Despite these minor misgivings, Christine was a boon to our family. Almost overnight, the atmosphere in the house changed. Christine took Meri's focus off of me, and some of the tension started to evaporate. Christine had grown up in the principle so she knew the joys and the pitfalls of plural marriage. She was incredibly cheerful and energetic, and she saw the world through rose-colored glasses. Her sunny disposition was the perfect antidote to the sour environment that had prevailed in our house for too long. As Kody likes to say, "Christine saved our bacon."

After a few months, Christine and Meri developed a camaraderie that allowed Meri to forget her grievances against me. I was able to take care of my baby and continue working. While Christine got her own apartment a few months after she and Kody were married, I still lived in the house like a roommate—but a lot of Meri's energy, both negative and positive, had been diverted to Christine.

Unlike Meri, who knew Christine from years back, I had no history with her. Once the dust settled between my sister wives, and they were able to put aside those initial petty jealousies that crop up at the beginning of almost any plural marriage, they spent a lot of time together. They had their own friendship, which I wasn't part of. They would run to the store together or go off on small adventures. I felt as if I was being purposefully excluded. I have always been overly sensitive to exclusion, even if I didn't want to be part of the activity I was being left out of. Most of the time, when Meri and Christine were going off to do their own thing, I wouldn't have wanted to go on account of Logan. However, the simple fact that I wasn't being invited abraded me. Groups of three women are often difficult. Someone always feels as if she is getting shortchanged even if it's all in her imagination. Initially, when Christine joined the family, this person was me.

Once the bond between Christine and Meri was cemented, Meri was much less difficult to get along with. Our lives became more peaceful. I got a decent job at a government agency with good pay and started to feel a little more confident about my career path. While Kody and I still hadn't eased into what most people would consider a conventional marriage—one based on romantic love—we had developed a highly functional relationship. We communicated well with each other and we complemented each other on an intellectual level.

Not long after I had Logan, Christine and Meri each bore their first children, Aspyn and Mariah. We started off on the greatest adventure of our lives—parenting an ever-growing brood of wonderful kids. A greater sense of camaraderie sprung out of raising our children together. Becoming parents as one family became the most essential part of our lives and the most defining trait of our family life.

I think that when Christine and Meri had their first children, they began to understand me a little better. After I had Logan, and before my sister wives had kids of their own, they didn't understand why I was tired so much of the time. They didn't understand my priorities. They thought I was complaining too much about trivial things, such as not having time to shower, do the dishes, or run errands. However, once their children were born, they were able to empathize with the challenges of motherhood and how having a child can complicate the simplest things. Once they grasped this, they were more willing to help me out. We were able to lean on one another and help to accomplish little tasks that motherhood makes difficult—cleaning, errands, talking on the phone in peace.

For the most part, Meri, Christine, and I were able to put aside our differences and create a warm and stable environment for our kids. We raised them as one family. While they may have separate mothers, they do not think of themselves as anything other than full siblings.

I loved coparenting our kids. I was able to work while Meri and Christine homeschooled the children who weren't sent to our church school. I felt safe and secure knowing that while I was out at the office, my children were receiving precisely the education and the care I wished for them. I never worried when my children were out of my sight. I trusted Meri and Christine to handle every situation and to make all parental decisions in my absence—in this regard, we were one team. I didn't have to be called on whether to administer cold medicine or not. I did not have to be called when Logan hit another one of the children. Christine and Meri handled it the way they knew I would want it handled. It was lovely.

When he was little, Logan was a daredevil. He got into everything. He was fearless. One afternoon, Meri had heated up some syrup and placed it in a pitcher on the counter. It was far out of the reach of any of our children. However, somehow Logan managed to rig up a contraption made from several chairs, which he climbed up to get his hands on the pitcher. He was too small to lift the pitcher and brought it crashing down on his head. The syrup scalded his forehead. Meri knew exactly what to do to minimize the burn. By the time I got home from work, there was only a small mark on Logan's face.

When you have as many kids as we do, these small traumas are not at all uncommon. Most of the time, when one of my kids got injured, I wouldn't find out about it until I got home from the office. By then, everything would have been taken care of by my sister wives. Whichever child had been hurt would be soothed, and the accident was already a fading memory.

My coworkers, most of whom didn't know I was polygamous, never understood why I was able to work late at a moment's notice. I was always at a loss to explain why I was so flexible regarding my home life. They didn't understand why I was never stressed about day care and grocery shopping, play dates and doctors' appointments for my kids. They couldn't figure out why I didn't need to rush home to fix dinner—or why I never, ever discussed what I was cooking. My coworkers thought I had the easiest life imaginable. Some of them even wondered if I was secretly wealthy—if you can imagine that! I didn't explain my situation, but I did hint that I had the best babysitters in the entire world.

From the day they were born, my children entered a rich, thriving environment with various outlooks to color the way they see and appreciate the world. For all of their lives they have had the benefit of four (now five) parents who expose them to a wide range of different interests, talents, and opinions. I know it is a cliché to say it, but if it does truly take a village to raise a child, my children have grown up in the best town in America.

I'm not good at arts and crafts, and my cooking and baking skills are not anything to boast about. As always, I prefer to lose myself in my work. So my major contribution to the family is financial and practical. Thankfully, my kids never suffered from having a mother who can't sew or bake. There are three other wonderful mothers in their lives who are creative and talented in areas in which I'm not, so my children never go without amazing Easter outfits or Halloween costumes.

If a birthday party were left up to me, I'd rush off to the supermarket on my way home from work and pick up a sheet cake with greasy blue roses. Thankfully, I have Christine in my family, who usually jumps at the chance to make something homemade. Even though Christine is extremely creative and generous with her time around the house, a lot of the time she flies by the seat of her pants. She's so carefree and silly that she can often overlook the most basic details, such as the need to put gas in the car!

I, on the other hand, am a worrier and a planner. I make my sister wives crazy with my plans and my contingency plans, and my contingency-contingency plans. Although these differences do lead to conflicts, they make our household a fun, dynamic place.

Even though I clash with Christine and Meri from time to time, I'm thrilled that my kids have had the benefit of both of their personalities. If they had grown up with just me, there would be so many things to which I wouldn't have exposed them. My sister wives have provided my kids with a wealth of experience, and they have helped me create six wonderful, well-rounded children.

About five years into our marriage, after Christine had joined the family and things had settled down somewhat, Kody began to mature emotionally. This change had a lot to do with the fact that Kody started taking charge of his own decisions. When Kody was new to polygamy, he often sought the counsel of elders who had grown up in the faith and now had plural families of their own. Among those he turned to for guidance were the members of Meri's family. Obviously, learning from those familiar with the faith and principle was crucial to Kody's development. However, no two families or situations are alike.

Eventually, Kody had garnered enough guidance from outsiders. When he began to rely on what was in his heart instead of primarily on the guidance of others, his emotional maturity began to show. He began to make decisions confidently, and he asserted what he wanted instead of what others told him to want. When this happened, he became a stronger leader in our household. He developed the confidence to take charge and stand on his own two feet.

While he still had a lot of responsibility with three wives and many little kids, he had grown into a profound sensitivity and consideration the likes of which I've never seen in any other man. I guess having three wives and many children taught him how to communicate with us in clear and loving ways—and he discovered how to devote himself to each of his marriages. He burst out of the fog in which he'd been wandering during those first tumultuous years, and became the most sensitive and caring husband and parent I could have thought possible. Without his maturation, our lives as one cohesive and coherent family would never have become what they are today.

Although Kody had matured significantly, and was no longer the naive, spontaneous romantic, with such a large family we still had trouble making ends meet. For much of the first decade of my marriage, I lived with either Meri or Christine. Our house was crowded, and paying the bills was always a challenge—we never had enough money no matter how hard we worked. This was the main point of contention in any argument I had with Kody. That, and we were practically on top of one another in our small house. There wasn't any room to breathe or think.

Kody did the best he could, and I never once doubted his commitment to me or to our children. Whenever I expressed my grievances, Kody would always remind me, "I'm committed. I'm not going anywhere." I knew he never would. He was the one and only stalwart in my life and the best and most hands-on father I'd ever seen.

During the eighth year of our marriage, I gave birth to my fifth child, Gabriel. Afterward, I sank into a horrible postpartum depression. I felt overwhelmed by having had so many children in quick succession, and felt seriously depressed at our lack of financial means. I knew I was miserable, but had no idea how to fix the situation.

I also had a particularly nasty fight with Meri—one of the worst we'd ever had. I was at my breaking point. I couldn't see my way out of my depression. I told Kody that I was leaving. That night, I got in the car and drove to my mother's house.

The next morning, Kody picked me up to run errands with

him. While we were driving, he nonchalantly asked me, "So, are you better now?"

His failure to understand how low I was felt like a slap in the face. Part of me wanted to scream and part of me wanted to laugh at his ignorance and his hopefulness that everything had become better overnight. That afternoon, I bundled all the kids into the car and took them to my mom's. I had reached rock bottom.

Until this point, the majority of my struggles within my family arose from sharing a living space. For several years I had had the means to move out and into my own place, if I'd been willing to turn my back on contributing financially to the family—but I wasn't. When we all came into the principle, we looked down on plural families that didn't live together. We believed that living as a unit made us stronger and allowed us to achieve necessary personal and spiritual growth quicker. As we saw it, living under one roof was the only way to do things. We had swallowed this ideal completely. So despite my struggles within the family, I was unwilling to give up on this vision that I'd held onto since I accepted polygamy.

However, after that fight with Meri, I'd had enough. My kids and I stayed with my mother for several months, until I found my own place. My job paid a decent salary, which allowed me to buy a better car, in addition to my own home. I started to build a life for myself apart from the sisterhood.

I wanted my identity as an individual apart from the family, and to achieve that, I needed my own house. I also knew that if I left our shared space, I wouldn't be leaving the marriage or the family—Kody would have done anything he had to in order to keep us all connected, in one house or many.

Soon after I got my own house I made one of the most important decisions of my life—I went back to school and got a degree in accounting. Getting a degree changed my world. I didn't realize how badly I'd wanted to do something like this. I felt personally and intellectually fulfilled. I was also certain that my career would thrive. This sense that I was taking control of my life and my future gave me invaluable self-confidence.

While I was living on my own, I was in no way cut off from the family. After a while, Kody began staying at my house on our nights together. I was also determined that my children should not feel separated from their siblings. During the day I would drive them nearly thirty miles to Christine and Meri, who would provide day care and homeschooling. On the weekends, we would get together for family meals.

Yet the separation did wonders for me. I was able to run my household as I wanted, not as my sister wives suggested. Before marrying Kody, I had always done the dishes in the morning, leaving my evenings free for relaxation. This habit—which in my mind is certainly not a bad one—drove my sister wives crazy. They insisted that I clean up at night, which irked me. Things like this may seem trivial, but over the years, small differences can really fester and come to stand for larger issues. But now, on my own, I didn't have to worry about what anyone else thought. I could leave the dishes in the sink overnight as I liked. I could do things as they pleased me.

In addition to being able to indulge my housekeeping habits, having my own place allowed me to focus on work and on school. And perhaps because I was so busy, I didn't have time to think about the petty stuff that was the source of so many of my earlier grievances with Meri. We moved on. Meri, Christine, and I each had our own home. We had our own kitchens—always a major source of strife—and could live as we liked without interference or comment from the others.

My happiness and my independence allowed Kody and me to enter a new phase in our relationship. I know it sounds silly to say, but after ten years of marriage, we finally had the time to get to know each other on a more spiritual and intimate level—and to enjoy our moments alone. We became parents so soon into our marriage that we rarely had time to ourselves. When we finally did, it was refreshing and reassuring. I felt that my marriage was stronger than ever.

Two years after I'd established myself in my own house, Kody told me that he was moving the family to Utah. He had found a job for which he wouldn't have to travel. He would be home with his kids every night.

"Okay," I told him. "See you later."

No way was I going to give up the peace and independence I had found. I had a great job. I had a great house. I wasn't leaving, and most of all, I wasn't going to live with my sister wives under one roof again. I worried about what would happen if we all lived together once more. I was stubborn. I stood my ground for almost a year. But soon I started to miss the family. And I knew that my children really missed living closer to their siblings.

As I was coming to this realization, Kody told me something that completely changed my mind regarding the move to Utah. He had found a house—a big house with three separate apartments, each with its own living quarters—kitchen, living room, and bedrooms. The house had seven bathrooms! It was a polygamous family's dream. This was all I needed to know. My kids could be reunited with their siblings on a permanent basis. I could be close to the family, yet still have my space.

I was delighted by this development. I had been alone for months, and I could no longer deny that I was incredibly lonely. I missed my family. I missed the everyday interactions, the liveliness, and the chaos. The fact that we could all live together, yet maintain separate living quarters, felt like a dream come true. And it turned out to be just that.

The big house changed everything. We were able to be together as a family in a natural and relaxed way. I had my own space, but my kids had their siblings and the other mothers in the same building. Most important, Kody was going to be home all the time. From the day Logan, our first child, was born, Kody has shown himself to be the best father any child could have hoped for. Now with the new house and his new job, he had the opportunity to see all of his kids on a daily basis. It was magical.

The new phase that Kody and I had embarked upon when I moved into my own house only grew sweeter in the big house. I had been so overrun with kids, my job, and my schooling that I had never allowed myself to be emotionally vulnerable to him. Throughout the first years of our relationship—especially when I was feeling unsure of my place in the family—I was determined to prove my self-sufficiency.

When I first met Kody, love was only about an intellectual connection and a friendship. I wanted a practical relationship that would provide a happy, stable environment for my children. That was enough for me. I am low maintenance when it comes to all things romantic. I prefer a good conversation and an afternoon spent together in a bookstore than all the hand-holding and sappy sweet talk in the world.

Nevertheless, I have a husband who is unbelievably sensitive to my needs and wants. He is intimately engaged with his children. He is the most logical, loving parent I've ever seen. So I'd lucked into the most romantic thing I could have ever dreamed of—an ideal parent with whom I also have an intellectual connection.

In the big house, I started to let down my guard and show Kody my more sensitive side. I felt confident in my place in the family, yet I had my own personal space. I have always been wary of being emotionally vulnerable. Because I'm afraid of being hurt, I throw up a wall and resist letting people in. In the big house, however, I found myself able to let him know when something was bothering me. I allowed myself to let him see when I was hurting and to help me if I needed it.

Kody and I have forged a life together from a strange and distant beginning. We continue to evolve as a couple, exploring a more tender and romantic side of our relationship. In many ways, you could say our love story is just beginning.

My relationship with Kody wasn't the only relationship that benefited from our move into the big house. Once I finished school and rediscovered my self-esteem, I stopped taking others' criticism of me so seriously. I had to learn that I wasn't going to let anyone tell me how I should act, what I should do, or how I should behave. And once I stopped listening to everyone else's voices in my head, I began to relax around my sister wives. We came to a mutual understanding and a collective respect for our similarities and differences.

We've done so much growing up together. And like real sisters, we can look back on our collective struggles—our major arguments and silly squabbles—and if not laugh at them, at least shrug them off. Now we can't even remember what half the fights were about. We've shared so much and been through a lot that with a word or a signal we can remind one another of an entire experience or story. We are bonded by our emotional history as well as our collective experiences.

Our life together, however, is still a day-by-day process. Every day we all have to check our natural reactions to things and temper them. We have to be careful not to say things to one another in a hurtful manner. Every decision we make has to be grounded in what is best for the entire family as a whole. It's complicated, but it's worth it because we've created something rich and intricate. If I were to lose one of my sister wives or one of her children, I would feel as if I had lost a limb.

Although Meri, Christine, and I are very different in our natures, we have grown to share the same values. The family we have now is an amalgam of each of our individual habits. We have all contributed something to the way our family runs. My sister wives have influenced the way I see the world, and I have done the same for them. Some of these changes are moral—we are, among our culture, considered fairly open-minded, almost liberal. And some of these changes are practical. For instance, if one of my sister wives prefers to feed her kids at seven and the other at five, we'll adopt six as our dinnertime. By adapting to and adopting one another's traits, we've developed our own culture.

One of the things I had to work on once I moved into the big house with my sister wives was not falling into the pitfall of comparing my relationship with Kody to theirs. Comparison is the death of plural marriage. It leads to debilitating unhappiness. For instance, if I see that one of my sister wives has apples, my instinct is to say that I want apples, even if what I really want is oranges. I have to be true to myself and admit what I want and not simply want something because my sister wife has it. I can't regress and say, "Kody, you love her more because you give her apples and I don't have apples." Our marriages are individual and we don't want or need the same things. But awareness of what someone else has in her relationship can cause you to question yours. And this is where the danger lies. Kody is tender with us in different ways. He has different methods of expressing his love. Maybe he leaves notes for one wife, sweet voice mails for another. Or maybe the way of showing his love is by always putting someone's kids to bed. These differences are vital to our lives. They are what make each of our marriages unique and special.

Somehow, after sixteen years, we had finally arrived at the ideal I'd envisioned when I'd accepted the principle. I was part of a happy, thriving family. We were able to make decisions as a group with a minimum of strife and bruised feelings. We had found our groove. I didn't think that anything could disrupt our flow.

I was fairly surprised when Kody came to me one afternoon and told me he was thinking about courting Robyn, but the way he handled it left me in awe of his emotional growth. He had learned so much from all the years with Meri, Christine, and me.

When Kody began to court Robyn, it became clear to me that he finally empathized with the difficulty I'd had coming into the family. He showed that he'd learned from my struggles, and was very careful about how slowly he integrated Robyn into our lives. He allowed her ample time to get to know each wife and all of our children individually. When they were getting to know each other, before they'd been given permission to court, Kody would bring one of the wives or several of the children down to St. George in southern Utah to spend a weekend with Robyn. In doing so, he made sure Robyn felt as if she was going to be an important part of our family—and he also let the family know that they were still as important as they'd been before Robyn came into the picture. He was very protective of Robyn, so that when they eventually married, she would feel as if she already belonged in our midst.

Kody and Robyn's courtship coincided with a huge development in our lives. After careful consideration—and endless family discussions—we decided to participate in a reality TV show about our family. This decision wasn't without complications. After all, there can be consequences when polygamists go public. But these unfamiliar waters certainly complicated Robyn's entry into the family. It drew out her courtship with Kody and forced their wedding to be put off for a few extra months.

I was completely fine with Robyn and Kody's courtship. It wasn't until after they got married that I started to struggle. It's hard to reconfigure your life—your needs and your children's needs—with a new wife in the picture. My mother explains this adjustment in a clever way. She say that wives are like spokes in a wheel—they keep the wheel balanced, grounded, and strong. When a new wife comes in, you all need to move over. It's an uncomfortable adjustment at first, but when you get your groove back you're stronger because of it.

Robyn brought three children into the family, which was an exciting change. We decided that a good way to integrate our families was to enroll our kids, many of whom had been home-schooled, in a public school along with Robyn's kids. There are, of course, some parenting differences between the way we raised our children before Robyn arrived and the way Robyn brought her kids up. Since Meri, Christine, and I had so many children, we didn't have the time or the space to baby them. If something didn't go their way, tough. Get up, brush yourself off, get onto the next thing. We're not catering to you.

Robyn coddles her children more, which is certainly understandable given their previously tumultuous home life. So we are learning from her and she is learning from us. This, like many things in our household, is a work in progress.

They most important thing Robyn has taught us is how to argue in a more effective and polite manner. With such a chaotic household, there are going to be a lot of family discussions. Sometimes these can become heated and they blow up. Before Robyn came into the family, our arguments would often end unresolved with raised voices and slammed doors. Frequently, we were all worse off after a family discussion than before. So from time to time, it seemed worthless to discuss anything at all.

Early on in their relationship, Robyn and Kody got into an argument. However, through example, Robyn showed him how to take the time to talk a problem out and not walk away from it before a comfortable resolution has been reached.

These days, it is often Robyn who takes the lead in our family discussions. She keeps a cool head and navigates us through difficult waters. She never lets us leave the room until we've settled an issue. Thanks to Robyn, we are able to avoid bruised feelings and the long periods of unhappiness that used to follow our family talks.

Even though Robyn brought so much into our family, during the few months after she married Kody, I felt as if I were wearing shoes on the wrong feet. Our rhythm was disrupted, and I'm afraid we were all a little brutal on her. Robyn went out of her way to extend olive branches to me. She'd offer to help me with the kids' homework on crazy days. She would pick up little trinkets or knickknacks that symbolized our family and offer them as "just because" gifts. Robyn collects Christmas ornaments, and her first Christmas with the family, she selected unique ornaments to give to each of us.

Regardless of Robyn's efforts, during the first year, I was unwilling to accept her offers. I was settled in my ways and not open to anything new. Despite my spiritual witness, I found myself kicking and kicking against opening myself up to Robyn. I was certain she and Kody were destined to be together and that she was an essential part of our family. But I found myself unwilling to make the effort to build a bridge between us. As I learned during my initial months in the principle, just because something appears celestially destined doesn't make it easy.

When Robyn joined the family, I was very busy with my kids and my job. I was hardheaded and believed that I didn't have time or need for this new person. I imagined Robyn and I could live as if we were riding in the same car but looking out separate windows. I had worked hard to find equilibrium with Christine and Meri, and the three of us had formed our own sort of partnership. As far as bringing Robyn into the family, I didn't have any reservations. I just hadn't committed to the necessary emotional and practical work involved. I wasn't sure that I needed or wanted to make room for a new person in my life, despite the fact that I felt spiritually convinced she should marry Kody.

But after a while, I got tired of fighting against Robyn and the potential friendship between us. I finally understood how helpful she had been in teaching our family how to communicate better. I realized that I was looking for a way to "punish" Kody and Robyn for disrupting my life—and it took way too much time and energy to be angry with this woman who was trying so hard to open up to me. So I started letting her in. We still have a long way to go, but we've begun the journey. I am already starting to see the benefit of developing a relationship with Robyn. Before Kody told me that he had met Robyn and wanted to court her, I never had any vision of her as part of our lives. I was satisfied with our adult unit of four. I never saw her coming. Yet when Kody mentioned her for the first time, I felt spiritually moved. Now that she's here, it seems as if she was always meant to be here.

Robyn possesses an amazing amount of emotional maturity. One of the things that she has helped with in our family is pointing out areas in which all of the marriages need solidifying. She has helped Kody realize where he may be inadvertently shortchanging one of his other relationships. This, in turn, has given Kody the tools to explain to me that we need to demonstrate more warmth and affection in our marriage. I'm learning to be less pragmatic about love and more romantic, even if it's something as simple as not dashing out the door in the morning before Kody and I have had a good-bye hug.

Over the years, Kody and I fell into the unfortunate habit of letting family business and finances dominate our alone time. These became the only things we ever talked about. Since I'm completely work-oriented, it didn't seem strange to me to discuss business matters on our dates. The fallout of this was that eventually Kody and I stopped talking to each other as husband and wife. Instead, we interacted like business partners. We'd forgotten about the sweeter side of our marriage.

Something was clearly wrong. We both understood we needed to make a change. I recognized that I needed to change my tone with him and relearn how to talk sweetly and lovingly. I began to understand that I could have a more profound, caring, and emotional relationship with my husband if we put aside all the business chatter during our evenings together. Once I started doing this, I discovered that there is unlimited potential to enrich our relationship. As a result, our marriage has grown deeper and more caring than I'd ever imagined it could be—or even knew that I wanted it to be.

Just like Kody's and my individual relationship, our entire family is still evolving. We are learning more about one another every day. This is the beauty of the principle—it demands that you never stop working on yourself in order to be the best person you can be on this earth. There is no room for complacency. Naturally, there are bad days. There are times when I've said to my sister wives in the middle of a fight, "I would never be friends with you. Ever! If it were possible, I'd hate you." But I don't hate them, not at all. You don't pick your sisters. Sometimes you get along with your sisters and sometimes you want to kill them. But deep down, you always love them. Always.

Chapter Seven

CHRISTINE

The first year of Kody's and my marriage was tough. I realized that I hardly knew the man I married. I don't mean to say that I didn't love him. But he felt like a stranger to me. And I realized that I was completely unsure where I stood with him, which was a terrible and unsettling feeling.

I wasn't entirely unaware of the struggles I might face. Growing up around so many polygamous families, I was well aware of the problems and pitfalls—the anger and jealousy, as well as the daily organizational and financial struggles. I knew that the situation I was entering was going to be challenging. I'd never seen my parents fight, but I realized that once they got divorced, their marriage must have been troubled for a long time. But in our family, if you had a problem, you just put on a smile and didn't let it show. I never saw my parents try to work through their differences until it was too late.

But when I married Kody, I ignored any potential problems. I put on my rose-tinted glasses and cheerful disposition and imagined that when I entered a plural marriage, I wouldn't experience those issues other people faced. If I was naive, it was because I chose to be.

Not long after I married Kody, I stopped being able to cover my problems with a smile. I was nervous and insecure. I felt overwhelmed by my new situation. Janelle had just given birth to Logan. At first, the four of us—Meri, Janelle, Kody, and myself—couldn't agree on how to organize our household and raise the first child. Naturally, Kody doted on Logan. But this made me feel insignificant. How could I compete with a firstborn son?

For the first three months of my marriage, I lived in the house with my sister wives. It was a strange transition. However, despite some of my own struggles, I felt that the four of us were developing a solid family identity. We'd often eat meals together around a small kitchen table. I had grown up in a large family, filled with kids. I thought it was really, really strange to be sitting around a table with only adults for company.

Eventually, I realized that I needed to develop and deepen my relationship with Kody. I still didn't know him very well. Although I always idealized the notion of living with sister wives, it became clear that I required a little separation for a time. (Plus I'm sure my sister wives were getting sick of living with a couple of newlyweds!) So I got my own cottage. I loved that cottage. Kody and I needed some time together in our own world. We'd barely had a moment alone since we married.

Three months into our marriage, I became pregnant. Between my insecurities and my hormones, I was a wreck. For the first time in my life, I was apart from my parents and my friends. I was living in Wyoming, which was cold, bleak, and far away from home. I was lonely and worried about my marriage. I tried talking about my problems with Kody, but I didn't know how to express myself. I didn't have the vocabulary for telling him what was wrong.

Kody didn't know how to listen to me. During our first fight, which was, predictably, about the fact that I thought he divided his time unfairly between his wives, he just put his head in is hands and covered his face. It was as if he was trying to make it all go away. He didn't have the emotional tools to deal with the needs of three wives. I knew that he felt he had married me too soon. The four of us were too young to deal with the situation we'd created.

Not long after Logan was born, Janelle went back to work. She was the most employable member of our family and was able to get the best jobs. While she worked, I looked after Logan, which was a joy and a delight. I loved mothering him. It was the highlight of that first difficult year.

Kody likes to say that I was instrumental in Logan's first year. Since Meri and Janelle were still struggling with each other, I was able to bring joy into his world. I created a sort of truce between my sister wives, which made the house more peaceful and loving for Logan. Logan is certainly the child of all three mothers. Meri provided constructive discipline, Janelle, a safe and comfortable place. And despite my own problems, I showed him as much happiness and joy as I could. I played with him as much as possible, teaching him both silly and instructional games.

While I enjoyed taking care of Logan, I spent the majority of my first pregnancy down in the dumps. I had lost sight of who I was. Like Janelle, when I married Kody and entered an already established family, I lost my identity. I was no longer my bubbly, energetic self. I couldn't look on the bright side because I was unable to see the bright side. Even though I had a strong testimony in plural marriage and always wanted to enter a family as a third wife, it was harder than I thought it would be. I struggled with my disappointment and frustration that something I thought would be perfect—celestial even—was actually hard work and brought about a certain amount of pain. Before marrying Kody, I honestly believed that being a third wife would be the easiest position because the family would have already worked through all their issues regarding jealousy and sharing. But I had no understanding of how much work would be left to do.

Right after my first child, Aspyn, was born, I got a phone call from an old friend back in Utah.

"Christine," she said, "where are you right now?"

I didn't understand her question. I told her that I was in Powell, Wyoming, where I lived.

"I know where you are physically," she said. "But where are you emotionally? You seem lost. You don't seem like yourself," she said. "What's changed?"

I told her I no longer felt good or worthy. I felt insecure in my marriage, which was about the worst feeling in the world.

"You're still the same girl you've always been," my friend said. "And that's the reason Kody married you. Kody loves you for you. Don't change. Don't mope. And don't try and be anyone different."

For some reason, her words really resonated with me. I was a wife and a mother, and I knew I could be happy if I wanted. I'd lost my identity only because I'd let it happen. I could be me and be happy if I chose. I know this sounds overly simplistic, but all I needed was for someone to remind me that it was up to me to reclaim my sense of self. I needed a kick in the pants. After all, I was the one who'd committed to the plural lifestyle. I was the one who had wanted sister wives more than I'd wanted a husband. It was up to me to enjoy it and make it work.

Once I became more relaxed, I began to understand my place in the family. I started becoming an active and important force in negotiating a truce and soothing a lot of our hurt. Meri and Janelle didn't have a relationship at all, but I had started to develop a fun sort of camaraderie with Meri. In addition to this, I was able to talk to Janelle about her interests and concerns.

I'd always idealized the nature of sister wives. I expected that they would be my best friends. After that first troubling year, I realized that friendships aren't instantaneous. If you want someone to be your best friend, you have to work on the relationship.

Over time, I was able to forge close friendships with Meri and Janelle. Meri became my best friend. Janelle and I grew extremely close, but since she is much more reserved than either Meri or me, our friendship is slightly less dynamic and more practical—which doesn't mean I love her any less than I do my other sister wives.

After Aspyn was born, I started to benefit from the sister wife experience I'd always hoped for. Aspyn was the first girl and a true delight. She helped restore my sense of happiness and joy. I was a mother and a wife—equally important as my sister wives. Once I'd given birth, I began to lose a tremendous amount of weight. I guess my puppy fat was ready to melt off with the pregnancy pounds. (Although I have to admit, I am the cutest pregnant woman in the world!) One day after I'd slimmed down, Kody, Janelle, and I were out shopping. We were in a clothing store where everything was far out of our price range.

Money was really tight then. (It often is in our family.) We may have been married and had kids, but we were as financially secure as a group of teenagers. I was looking around the store and I found this white fringe outfit that I just had to try on. When I came out of the dressing room, Janelle said, "Christine, you have to buy that."

I protested that it was too expensive.

The outfit cost a hundred dollars, which is more than any of us had ever spent on anything besides rent in our lives. It was ridiculous. But I thought I looked pretty cute in it—and Janelle and Kody clearly agreed.

"I don't care," Kody said. "I'm buying that for you."

Moments like this, away from the duties of family life, proved to me that the possibility of a fun and tranquil plural family was indeed within our reach.

We had been moving around a lot since I came into the family. I had my own place for a while, as did Janelle, but for financial reasons, right after Aspyn was born, we had all moved back into one house. Shortly after this, Meri gave birth to her daughter, Mariah.

The house was cramped with four adults and three children in diapers. Kody was miserable at work. While we tried our best to work on all our relationships with one another and learn how to raise our children, our close living situation made tempers rise. Kody decided we needed a change. We needed to get out of Powell. So we moved from a one-thousand-square-foot house in Wyoming to a three-thousand-square-foot house in Utah. This house was a major change for us. We had both a kitchen and a kitchenette. This meant that Janelle no longer had to share a kitchen with Meri and me—something that had always been a source of strife among the three of us.

When we got to Utah and settled into our new, larger house, we were able to relax a little. We had, quite literally, more breathing room. Since our daughters were born only a few months apart, the relationship between Meri and me began to deepen. Janelle was able to get her career, which had floundered a little in the tiny town of Powell, back on track. This made her unbelievably happy. I had a part-time job, which brought in a little essential money. But most of all, I was a stay-at-home mom.

Meri and I share a lot of common interests, such as cooking and crafts. Since we like to cook the same sort of food, we worked well in the kitchen together. We also love planning family outings and holidays. We often arranged family excursions so we'd have the opportunity to take tons of photos of the kid in different locations.

We spent a lot of time sewing our children matching outfits. Around Christmastime, we'd dress up the kids and pile them into the car and drive them to the photo studio for holiday pictures. This was always a chaotic adventure, but well worth it.

Our holiday preparations, especially for Christmas and Thanksgiving, were intense. We would start planning months in advance. We organized meals, decorations, activities, gifts, outfits, and surprises for everyone in the family.

Once we moved to Utah, things began to look up. We were happy parenting and working. It was during this period that Kody and I began to discover each other. Now that things had settled down, we had the space and the freedom to get to know each other in a deeper and more spiritual sense. We were also able to start having fun—something that was essentially missing during the first year and a half of our marriage. We loved spending time with Aspyn. We marveled over how special she was to us. We spent hours playing with her, guessing at the challenges we'd face as parents. We often discussed all the kids we wanted to have together. We got to know each other by sharing the dreams we had for our children's futures. Talking about the family we wanted really cemented our bond and made us remember the love that was the foundation of our marriage.

A year after we returned to Utah, both Janelle and I had our second children, Madison and Mykelti. Suddenly there were five kids in diapers in one house. You would have thought that the chaos would have been too much for us, but the joy of our growing family trumped any domestic issues.

What really brought us together and made us more functional is that not long after we moved to Utah, Kody finally found a job he enjoyed. Kody's new position required him to attend trade shows, one of which was in Nauvoo, Illinois. This trip would require him to be on the road for two weeks, towing his trailer with his materials and displays. Both Meri and Janelle had been on trips with Kody, but I'd never had the opportunity. When Kody asked me to go, I was over the moon. He could have taken anyone and he took me! I suddenly felt special again.

This trip was a huge turning point in our relationship. It was the first time we had spent so much time alone together—just us and our daughters, Aspyn and Mykelti. In many ways the trip was a disaster—the car overheated, we had to keep the kids cool by feeding them ice chips. We broke down numerous times. But these hardships only brought Kody and me closer together. No matter how difficult things became, I was prepared to sing songs of joy the entire way. I loved every minute of the adventure at Kody's side. Although our drive was similar to pulling a handcart through the desert, I couldn't wipe the smile from my face. I think Kody really dug my positive attitude. Every time I glanced at him, he looked so cute and sweet. Instead of suffering in the heat, he was beaming.

I had loved Kody since before we were married. I suspected that he had been falling in love with me for years. But on that trip is when Kody finally and irrefutably decided that he would step in front of a train for me—which is what he told me when we returned home. That trip was our true honeymoon experience. We had come so far since our "official honeymoon" when I worried that I'd married too quickly to a seemingly distant man I loved but didn't really know. Now I was certain that we were soul mates.

At the end of the trip, we turned to each other and said, "I know that I can trust you to be an amazing and incredible person for the rest of our lives together. I know that I will always be there for you and do everything possible to make things better for you." This was our commitment to each other. We both knew then that if and when disaster should strike, we would hold each other and look into each other's eyes and tell each other that we are glad for every second we spent together.

For many years, I felt that our lives were perfect. I loved being part of the family. I loved homeschooling the kids and taking care of the household. I received all the benefits that I'd expected from a plural marriage.

My other mothers had provided so much for me when I was growing up that the prospect of raising many, many kids together was precisely what I had in mind when I accepted the principle. For more than a decade, I had two best friends with whom I had the pleasure of rearing a wonderful household of children.

In many ways, I feel that I kept the household running by taking care of so many of the practical affairs. For years, I enjoyed this position. I loved being the primary stay-at-home mom. I cooked and cleaned. I had a garden and I canned. Since both Meri and Janelle worked, if Kody had a problem, something that needed to be done or fixed, I took care of it.

I prided myself in being there for everyone all the time. I tried to make sure that all the holidays and birthdays were special. Whenever we had family functions, my house had to be perfect, the food had to be perfect. I needed to create the ideal environment for what I believe is our perfect family.

While I was doing all of this, I began to teach at our church school part-time. Then I joined the board of the Sunday school and taught a Sunday school class. I also became an academic adviser. The church and the home are the most important places in our lives, and I needed them to be perfect, too.

Then one day I realized I was overwhelmed, too stressed out by all that I'd taken on. I hadn't noticed, but for a while I'd been unable to give 100 percent to anything I did. Unintentionally, I'd started letting everything slip.

Around this time, Kody and I decided to have another baby. I realized that I could stop holding everything together and do the one thing I always wanted to do—be the best mom possible. My kids are the most important thing in my life and I know that I would never be comfortable if I wasn't completely there for them.

During my pregnancy, I decided to give up all nonmaternal duties. I stopped teaching. I told my family I was very stressed out and needed to take some time off from everything but being a mom. For nearly fifteen years, I'd devoted myself single-mindedly to preserving everyone else's happiness, but now I needed to restore mine.

There was another factor that led to this drastic reconfiguration of my place in the household. About a year before I became pregnant with Truely, I had a devastating argument with Meri. For a while, I'd been feeling that she was too tough on my kids. While I understand that all children need discipline, I often felt that she went too far when it came to my children. It seemed to me that she was taking her frustrations out on my kids in particular. As a result of this, many of them were wary of her and were afraid to cross her accidentally.

I let this situation go on too long, and I let my emotions well up. Instead of talking to Meri calmly and explaining what I'd observed her doing and how she might fix her behavior, I exploded. I yelled and screamed and told her to stop talking to my kids and to stop interfering in their lives. Since I'm afraid of confrontation, I always allow stuff to build up till it's too late. So instead of trying to work it out with Meri, I just shut her out.

This argument shattered my world and made me realize that I have always had superficial relationships with people. I've always tried to ignore problems by putting on a brave face and keeping people at a distance. This fight made me realize that I'd never honestly opened up to Meri and Janelle, but had forged our friendships out of a need to cement the sister wife ideal I'd envisioned.

After our fight, Meri and I stayed out of each other's way. We no longer sought out each other's company to watch movies or just hang out. When circumstances brought us together, we were never openly rude or hostile. We maintained a level of cordiality. But the warmth was gone.

To this day, we are still working on becoming closer again. It has been a slow process of starting to feel comfortable being open and honest with each other. We have had to learn how to immediately tell one another if we feel offended by something. We still do not have the wonderfully close relationship we used to share. I know we will continue working on it though. My relationship with Meri is very important to me. I'm certain she feels the same way about me.

After my fight with Meri, I realized that the only people I'd ever let in were my mother and Kody. My mother broke my heart by divorcing my father and leaving our faith. About a year after the argument, we met Robyn, and even though I welcomed her into my family, it shook my foundation and left me unsure of whether I could trust Kody's commitment to our marriage.

The four of us—Meri, Janelle, Kody, and I—had been a nearly perfect unit for almost sixteen years of near absolute bliss. Over that time, there had been minor discussions of potential courtships, but nothing ever came of it.

I had grown used to being the last wife. I *loved* being the last wife. Kody and I had a tremendous relationship. He was my best friend and my closest confidant. Since Meri, Janelle, and I all served entirely unique functions in Kody's life, I had never had cause to be jealous of his relationships with my sister wives. (My fights with them never had anything to do with Kody.) I knew that Kody's relationships with both of them were great. And I knew that what I brought to him and to the family was different from any other wife. I was entirely secure and at peace regarding my marriage and my importance in Kody's world. Jealousy had simply never, ever been part of my life. But when a fourth woman entered the picture, this changed.

Growing up polygamous, I'd watched other women go through the experience of getting new sister wives. I never understood their jealous reactions. Whenever they complained about the domestic upheaval caused by a new wife, I wanted to tell them, "It's all part of the principle. You're just being a baby," or, "Feeling jealous is a choice. You are choosing to be jealous. Get over yourself." I should have listened to my own counsel! I didn't understand how hard it could be.

I really feel that I owe Robyn an apology. In many ways, I betrayed her. Before she and Kody were courting, I was really enthusiastic about her and I wanted her to love our family—and to love me. I went out of my way to show her our best side. The first time Robyn came over to our house, I made sure we had a big meal ready. I put as much effort as I could into welcoming Robyn with open arms. We have such a wonderful family, and I wanted to ensure that she had no choice but to fall for all us.

However, when she and Kody courted and married, I was no longer the sweet person Robyn first met. The loving sister wife I'd initially promised her disappeared. I feel guilty for offering something to Robyn I couldn't provide. I felt as if I'd lied to her. If I did, it was through no fault of Robyn's but entirely due to my own problems. I feel blessed in knowing that Robyn is generous enough to forgive me.

Kody and Robyn's courtship came at a time of huge personal upheaval. I was pregnant with Truely, and we had also entered new and uncharted territory as we began filming *Sister Wives* for TLC. When Kody started courting and then married Robyn it really rocked me. I gave birth to Truely and was suffering from extreme postpartum depression. I never thought I'd feel such a sense of loss and such crippling jealousy. I thought I was better and stronger than that. I really did.

The strangest thing is that I had a stronger testimony that Robyn should be part of our family than I ever did about whether I should marry Kody myself. I was certain, beyond a shadow of a doubt, that marrying Robyn was the right thing to do. I recognized immediately what an awesome, special, and wonderful person she was. She belonged in our lives. I knew that she and Kody deserved each other. And this is what made it so hard.

Despite my testimony that Kody courting Robyn was the right thing to do, I could not curtail my own insecurity that Kody was abandoning me for someone else. The undeniable fact about our lifestyle is that no matter how strongly committed to it you are and how much you long for sister wives, it is difficult to keep your petty jealousies in check. It was apparent that Kody and Robyn shared a destiny—but I couldn't help but feel that this might marginalize my place in Kody's life.

If Robyn had been a lesser woman—not as emotionally and spiritually intelligent, not as strong or as generous—I might not have been threatened by her. As ungenerous as it is to say, I could have, at least in part, disregarded her. But Kody didn't deserve a "lesser" woman. And I never would have allowed him to marry someone who wasn't as wonderful as Robyn.

During Robyn and Kody's courtship, it was evident to me how wonderful she and Kody were together and how much in love they were. I felt abandoned by my best friend and as if, once more, I'd lost my identity. I couldn't see myself as Kody's wife. Instead, I felt inconsequential, as if I'd been pushed to the side. It's a horrible feeling when you let someone in, allow him to become the most important person in your world, and then he replaces you. When this happened, I began to demand more of Kody, which was hard for him. He had started courting Robyn, so he had less to give me. Or at least that's what it felt like. Nevertheless, despite my own hurt, I have to hand it to Kody. When it comes to bringing in other wives and making everyone feel safe and secure with the transition, he has done a superb job.

During Kody's courtship of and marriage to Robyn, I felt that I needed more from him than he was giving me. He couldn't love me enough or spend enough time with me. Nothing he did satisfied me. I was so panicked about being neglected that I wanted more, more, more. I nagged and nitpicked. I felt it was his responsibility to do all the heavy lifting in our relationship.

I have to admit that during that period, I wasn't a lot of fun to be around. Eventually, Kody had enough. I was venting to him once about some way in which I felt I was being shortchanged, and he just looked at me and said, "I just want my best friend back. I need you. I miss you and want you back." There were tears in his eyes.

When I realized he wasn't saying it to be hurtful (which, by the way, was totally stupid to think!), I began to change, and to take the advice I'd so blithely given other women living plural marriage.

During the period I was taking out my own unhappiness and insecurity on Kody, I learned a lot from my kids. Kids being kids, they can whine and complain. They can nitpick and pester me about the smallest, most inconsequential thing. When they test me to the max, I can no longer deal with being around them. So I send them to their rooms. Suddenly, I realized that what my kids were doing to me, I was doing to Kody. I needed to stop harassing him and making demands on him. I had to let myself love him and let him love me. I, too, wanted my best friend back.

It's been a big change for me from being the person people could rely on for holidays and family meals to becoming the dependent one. During my struggles with postpartum depression and my own issues with making room for a new wife, I had to ask my sister wives to take over some of my duties—to organize family meals and trips, take care of the little kids during the day. I needed to lean on them while I rebuilt my own inner strength. Meri and I have gone a long way toward repairing our relationship. We have been traveling together, and I believe that we are back on track. But still, I'm hurting.

I've been very frank with Meri, Janelle, Robyn, and Kody about where I stand emotionally. I let them know what I need from them and what I can and cannot do. I recognize that they are always there for me, and everyone is supporting me now. I need their patience and their understanding. I will get through this, but I need time. I am lucky to have a wonderful, supportive husband.

As our family has become more settled, Kody has been more available to us as a group, taking on a leadership role in the day-to-day concerns that were once my chosen obligations. In many ways, this is more appropriate. He's made this transition wonderfully, which speaks to the amazing emotional maturity he's achieved over the years. I think he gets overwhelmed a little quicker than I used to, but he's learned to listen to all of us, to take our needs and problems into consideration, and then to apply them to the overall picture. I'm very happy to take a backseat while he does this.

Although Kody is a stronger man than he's ever been and grows more and more reliable every day, I feel a lack of stability in our own relationship. I can only blame myself and my insecurities for this. I will get through this only when I've strengthened my relationship with God. This will return my confidence to me. Then all of the jealousy will vanish and everything will fall into place.

I know that this will happen, because our family is incredibly strong. I've seen a lot of polygamous families in my life, and ours is the bomb! My own insecurities pale in comparison to our collective strength.

In the long run, I know my struggles are temporary. I have an amazing husband who is my best friend, and I have three truly incredible sister wives. Although there have been some rough periods, I never dreamed that it would be this great. Of all the examples of plural families I've seen, ours is truly the best.

Chapter Eight

ROBYN

When Kody and I got engaged, we didn't have enough money to get married or to help me move from southern Utah to Lehi. Janelle offered to let me move in with her, but I was desperate to avoid this situation. I needed time to explore my relationship with Kody. This would have been impossible living under the same roof as another wife. It wouldn't have been easy on anyone. I don't believe Kody would have been able to be as emotionally involved in our relationship had I been living with Janelle, nor would that situation have been fair on their marriage. So for the moment, I stayed put in St. George.

Even though we had no money to get married, Kody dreamed of a big, fancy wedding. It's his view that since polygamists marry so often, they don't value the marriage ceremony and the reception as they should. They don't do enough to make the day special. For the most part, polygamous weddings are humble. Kody swore that when he and I married, it was going to be a big deal.

While I love all the sweetness and romance attached to a big wedding, I didn't want all the bother and attention. And I certainly didn't want the drama I worried would come with the territory. The Browns had a comfortable and complicated family.

I didn't want to come storming in with a huge party and make myself the center of attention. I wanted a quiet yet romantic wedding. And I wanted it to happen as soon as possible. But no matter what size wedding Kody and I decided on, we were going to have to wait.

It was not entirely due to financial constraints that we were forced to put off our wedding. We got engaged at the end of September, and I was hoping that we could find a way to be married by December at the latest. My future sister wives were unhappy with this plan. When I discovered this, I knew that I was going to have to be incredibly sensitive to their feelings and wishes as I planned my wedding.

I quickly realized how foolish I'd been to consider getting married in December. I didn't want my wedding to Kody to distract from the Brown family's holidays. I didn't want my event to eclipse the children's Christmas. Getting married in January was also out of the question as it was Meri's birthday, Janelle's anniversary, and my son Dayton's birthday. February, too, posed similar problems.

While Kody and I were figuring out the best and earliest possible date for our wedding, the television show that he'd been discussing since we got engaged went from a dream to a reality. The show's producer, Tim Gibbons, sold a pilot to TLC. TLC was going to help us pay for our wedding. I knew that having a big ceremony meant the world to Kody. So I consented.

This immediately posed another problem. They wanted to open the show with our wedding. Kody and I vehemently objected to this. It would be a grave disservice to Kody's first three wives to feature his wedding to me in the opening episode of the show. Focusing on a new wife would shortchange their rich family history. Since the goal of the show was to exhibit the wonderful and wild Brown family, beginning with my story just didn't make sense. It would have been hurtful to all of those who'd built this family from the ground up. In addition to this, Kody worried that if the first thing the audience saw him do was get married, people would misinterpret his intentions and view him as "the marrying guy" instead of the family man he is.

After much discussion, Kody convinced the production team to begin the show with the core family and then introduce my story. This meant, once again, pushing back my wedding. Now my courtship would be extremely drawn out—and not only that, it would be filmed, something I'd never anticipated. I'm glad that Kody and I had time to ourselves before the cameras intruded into our lives. I'm sure that I wouldn't have gotten to know him had he been filming a show right from the start.

Eventually, we were able to settle on a date for our wedding at the end of May. When I began to plan the wedding, I wanted to involve my future sister wives as much as possible. I was aware that since TLC had become involved, the wedding was going to be a much larger event than I was comfortable with. And I worried that the amount of attention lavished on my wedding day might lead to hurt feelings within the family. I wanted to make sure that my special day was as much a celebration about my family as it was of my marriage. I wanted to do everything within my power to avoid offending my sister wives, some of whom didn't have the opportunity to have a large wedding. I had also watched other women in our church who were coming into a family not include the present wives in the reception and cel- ebration of their marriage. I had heard horror stories about these wives being hurt as they watched from the sidelines as the new wife married their husband. I was determined to make it a happy day for everyone.

While I was beginning to plan the wedding, Kody made a large commission on a sign he'd been trying to sell for ages. We used this money and my tax return to help me and my kids move into my own apartment in Lehi. This made planning the wedding infinitely easier. It also allowed me to start developing a closer relationship to my sister wives.

Of course, it would have been nicer for me to have been able to have a place either in or near the big house—not in one of the other wives' apartments, but in my own. This would have made me feel integrated into the family instead of feeling like an outsider. However, this was not possible, since the house was designed for a man with three wives, not four. I know a lot of people probably misinterpreted the fact that I was given my own house as my getting preferential treatment. This was not the case at all. There was simply no other reasonable option.

When I got to Lehi, I made it very clear to my sister wives that I wanted my wedding celebration to be about family. I made sure to include them in every step of the planning process—the flowers, the cake, the invitations, the food. In fact, Janelle even picked the location herself, which was great. My sister wives and I even went dress shopping for my wedding dress. The experience was really fun, and it was great to bond with them. I loved having their advice but I didn't find a dress. Later, I was looking by myself and was having trouble finding what would be appropriate. I had never been a plural wife before, so I was a little nervous about what to wear. Kody called right then and offered to help me, and I said yes. Later on in the show, Kody revealed this to everyone. I don't think he meant to cause any hurt feelings, but the damage was done. Janelle and Meri felt like I had pretended to want them involved in picking out my dress and then, behind their backs, had Kody help me instead. Christine's struggle was that Kody hadn't helped her pick out hers. I was frustrated with Kody for blurting out the story in a way that hurt my sister wives. I hadn't meant harm, I just needed to pick out my dress!

After I chose my colors for the wedding, I wanted each of my sister wives to have the exact style of dress she would like, but all in the same color scheme. Meri wanted to use the wedding as an opportunity to take a family portrait. I wanted this portrait to focus on the family, not on my wedding, so I had a second dress made to match my sister wives.

Although, I would have been happy with the smallest of receptions, the wedding was absolutely lovely. I really felt that it celebrated not just Kody and me, but the union of our beautiful families.

Sometimes I worried that it seemed as if I was getting preferential treatment. I got the big wedding followed by a long honeymoon. However, the honeymoon was both necessary and special to me. I never asked Kody for a ten-day trip, but he must have had a sixth sense that it was something important for us. Since we believe in remaining chaste before marriage, the honeymoon ushers in a new part of our relationship. Those ten days were especially important to me because of the hardships I had been through in my previous marriage. In addition to this, since I already had three kids, the minute we returned from our trip, Kody and I would be thrown into a cycle of homework and child care. We would be developing our relationship as a married couple with three younger children. So it was wonderful to have such an extended vacation from the cares of home and private time to build our relationship. It was comforting to know, however, that when I got back, my maternal duties would resume, but I would no longer be a single mother. I'd have a wonderful husband and three sister wives at my side.

I understand now that long my honeymoon was somewhat hurtful to my sister wives, who didn't have comparable experiences. I made sure Kody called all of them several times during our ten days away—but not all of my new sister wives took his calls. I found out later when we returned home how upset some of my sister wives were that Kody took a longer honeymoon with me than with them. I remember Christine talking to me and saying, "If you needed that long, just tell me. I need to know you needed it." I told her that I needed it but I didn't know how much until I was on the honeymoon with Kody—when you have been married and divorced, you can have the past come back to haunt you in the worst times.

Like many women who embrace plural marriage, I had an overly idealistic notion of how simple it would be to develop healthy and stable relationships with my sister wives. I understood that there had been some issues regarding my courtship, but I assumed when the wedding was over, these would be forgotten. I imagined that when I returned from my honeymoon, I'd easily slide into the Brown family. I thought the struggles my sister wives were going through would fade because Kody and I were now married.

Meri and I had started out with a really great relationship when I started courting Kody. I was so excited to see that she wanted me in her family. She wasn't just looking for a sister wife, she was looking for a best friend. I was overjoyed. She even pulled me into her room once and asked me what kind of ring and wedding I wanted because she would make sure it happened for me. It was my dream come true to know she cared about my happiness. Things seemed pretty good with Janelle and Christine as well. I was so excited to share a life and family with these three women. As the courtship progressed, Meri's and my relationship struggled, but I thought that once Kody and I were married that it would get better again. I knew Christine and Janelle were struggling, too, but again, I thought it would all get better once I was officially a part of the family and not just a fiancée, so I just held on.

When I chose to marry Kody, I wasn't just choosing him. I wanted a relationship with Meri, Janelle, and Christine. While Kody and I were courting, I wanted to be close to his three wives. Whenever I came over to their house or headed back to southern Utah, I would hug them hello or good-bye. I had felt secure that these women were open to my arrival in their family. After all, if they truly hadn't wanted Kody to marry again, it would have been simple for them to forbid it. A man must have absolute permission from his wives before considering a courtship with a new woman. Meri, Janelle, and Christine are an independent bunch and they put their family first. If they hadn't believed that I should be a part of their lives, they would have let Kody know. But even believing that I belonged in their family doesn't mean it was going to be easy for them to make room for me. That's a much taller order.

When I returned from my honeymoon, I was shocked to discover how much my sister wives were struggling. They were cold and standoffish and struggled to make room for me in the family. Where I had expected openness and acceptance, I found walls. Even though I was married to Kody, it still was very hard for them, so hard that they didn't know what to do with me. I felt as if my mere presence threatened them. No matter how hard I tried to be sweet or kind, it still wasn't enough. All my naive expectations that we would be best friends flew out the window.

Meri, with whom I'd once had a wonderful friendship, and I struggled a lot. She felt that anything bad going on between Kody and her was somehow my fault. This really hurt me since I had been ecstatic about the friendship I believed Meri and I could have. I didn't know how to repair our friendship, but I wanted so much to try. I loved Meri, and I wanted back what we had had in the beginning.

I really didn't anticipate how much my sister wives would struggle with me coming into the family. I was unprepared for the fact that they believed I was the source of their pain. I didn't understand how difficult making room for a new wife could be. I never, ever set out to hurt anyone. I found that simply having a relationship with Kody hurt them. Anything that he did for me had the potential of hurting them or making them jealous. I felt as if any kind of love and sweetness that they saw Kody and me share made them feel threatened and upset. So they shut me out.

There's a strange phenomenon that happens in our lifestyle. When you are struggling with jealousy and insecurities, you manage to transform your sister wife into some sort of monster. You begin to believe that your sister wife harbors you ill will or intentionally means to harm you. And from this paranoid perspective, real problems begin to arise.

Usually, this paranoia springs from an insecurity about your relationship, not with your sister wife but with your husband. Eventually, I discovered that some of my sister wives were often angry with me not because of something I'd done, but because they felt like Kody loved me more than them, and this scared and threatened them. When I learned this, I tried my best to open up a dialogue with whichever wife was struggling with me. By talking things out, I was able to gain a fuller perspective and realize that their issues with me were really not personal. Often, they struggle with me when they aren't feeling close enough to Kody, or when they are dealing with their own jealousy or insecurities. I feel these things myself, and I have to work on dealing with my own insecurities and jealousies and not blame my sister wives or Kody for them.

I know having a great relationship with my sister wives has less to do with them and me and more to do with them and Kody. In order for me to develop the friendships with them that I'd hoped and prayed for, I know that I need to promote their marriages, be a good friend and help them through whatever struggles they may be having, and, above all, support and love them.

After all, we are all women working toward the same goal: the strength and stability of our family and our marriages. We all want the same thing, and we don't want to hurt each other. Despite this knowledge, insecurity, which is the constant pitfall of our lifestyle, rears its ugly head. Instead of acknowledging that we are working together and that we want to make our family and friendships work, it can be tempting to think of your sister wife as the girl in high school who's fighting with you over your boyfriend.

Figuring out how to navigate our relationships is tricky. Even though some of us were raised polygamous, we still grew up in a monogamous world. Aside from our mothers' relationships with their sister wives, we don't really have much of a frame of reference for how to deal with the conflicts and the jealousy that crop up. After all, we never see relationships like ours on television, in movies, or read about them in books. We have to navigate our situation blindly, without a map or outside help.

I completely understand why my sister wives can be jealous of my relationship with Kody. Our marriage is fresh and young. They may sometimes believe that he loves me more than he loves them because of this, but that simply isn't true. I know Kody loves Meri, Janelle, and Christine. I wouldn't respect him otherwise.

I know, however, that the best thing for Kody's and my marriage in the long run will be for him to validate his other marriages and reaffirm his love for my sister wives. All our marriages go through high and low points, but he needs to commit to them and they to him so that together they will work things out. This is a universal truth in all marriages, polygamous or not. Although it's not always that simple, this is something I'm always bugging Kody and my sister wives to do. I want all the relationships in our family to be successful.

When things become difficult between me and my sister wives, they have a tendency to block me out and not give me a voice. While they might be jealous of my relationship with Kody, I don't think they realize how often I'm confronted with the fact that they all share a history that I will never be a part of. They have a culture within their family that was long established before I came in. They have stories, jokes, struggles, and triumphs that are simply off-limits to me. Sometimes it can be hurtful to know that although I'm married to Kody just as they are, I will never be as deeply entrenched in the family's history. I will always be the new kid on the block.

Sometimes it's challenging to speak up and ask my sister wives to make room for me in their world. I have been in relationships in the past where I've been steamrolled. After this happened, I made a promise that I would always stand up for myself. Since my sister wives had developed such a solid and preordained way of doing things before I arrived, there was a tendency to brush off my suggestions. I had to tell them that I deserve a voice in the family, too. However, since I wasn't around for those first sixteen years, my ideas and concerns often got downplayed.

During my first few months in the family, I would listen in family discussions while my sister wives and Kody would get angry with one another. I tried to suggest that there was a more constructive way of arguing—a safer, calmer way. I know from experience how much damage can be done when you don't have control of your anger and frustration. But the family pretty much told me that that they had their own way of doing things. Eventually, I showed them through example how to talk things out reasonably. Now I'm often asked to help mediate family talks.

My sister wives will sometimes try to mother me. I feel like I'm the "little sister wife." I have to remind my sister wives that I survived both a difficult marriage and several years of single motherhood on my own. I'm strong and independent. While I'm grateful for their advice, I don't always need it.

We're still in the process of blending our families. This has taken a great deal of patience. Before I arrived, the Brown family had their own way of running things, which was slightly different from mine. Since they have so many children, they cannot tend to all the discrepancies that arise. They have a saying: "If you're not bleeding, don't tattle." For the most part, they leave their children to work out their own problems.

I'm very emotionally sensitive to those around me, which makes it difficult to turn my back on even the smallest issue between two of our kids. If even the slightest disagreement arises, I want to get to the root of it. I want to sit the children down and talk it through, get to the source of the problem and solve it. Instead of telling the children to go work something out on their own, it's my instinct to mediate.

It is my nature to be emotionally in tune with everything around me, both bad and good. For instance, I'm careful to group our youngest girls in a way that one of them doesn't get picked on by the others for some of her quirks. I go out of my way to create an environment that is safe and protective for everyone in the family.

At first, the older kids and some of my sister wives thought I was babying my kids. I had to explain that I was just looking out for them—all of them, not just my own biological children. I had to explain to them that I raised my kids to be more emotionally sensitive to one another and to be comfortable expressing their problems and concerns. It's not a sign of weakness, I explained, to address your issues head on.

Soon some of the older children grew comfortable with my parenting style. They've begun to confide in me because they know I'm patient with their problems. They are willing to spill their guts to me about their most personal issues, which is something of a relief for them. I want not just all the children but all of my sister wives to feel that I am emotionally available to them, so they can talk to me about anything.

During the first year of my marriage to Kody, my sister wives began to recognize what they call my "emotional intelligence."

When I first started courting Kody, my viewpoint gave him a new perspective on his family and some of his relationships. At first, I think it was hard for my sister wives to hear my voice coming through when Kody spoke, but I think as time passed, my opinion was respected more and more. Janelle has expressed to me that she is grateful for my ability to make a tough conversation safe. Meri also confides in me when she is working through an issue because she knows I will validate her feelings.

After Kody and I got married, Meri and I decided to see a counselor together. We both wanted to get our relationship to the great place from which we'd started. I was heartbroken that we weren't close because it was all I wanted. Meri was very mature about facing tough issues with me. It has made us better people and better sister wives. I love Meri so much. From the moment I met her on my cousin's lawn, I felt an eternal connection to her. Meri is loyal, fun, and good. I love spending time with her. We have a lot of fun hanging out and being girls together.

We've both worked hard to implement the things we have learned in our relationship. She and I have repaired our bond and we've finally arrived at a place where we have our own friendship independent of the family. Now I tease her by telling her she tricked me into marrying her husband and then abandoned me! We have come so far that we can actually laugh at this. I'm so excited about the life that lies before us.

The potential for an everlasting friendship with these women is the best thing our faith has to offer. Meri and I have come so far in our relationship, and I am so grateful to have such a special closeness with her. I'm on the path to developing a closer relationship with Janelle and Christine as well. Janelle and I have opened the lines of communication and we have found that we have many things in common. She has amazing talents. I hope she knows how much I support her. Christine and I are building the foundation to a better relationship. Some days I know just to let her be where she's at. I miss it when she isn't her fun-loving self. I pray all the time that she understands I have her best interests at heart, and that I love her.

I want to do girl stuff with them all. I want to be close to them all. I love them all unequivocally. I want them to know that I will always be open to hearing what is bothering them so that we can get closer. I want to share our families' triumphs and sorrows with them. I want to support our husband together as a unified team.

I know that the potential for this closeness is there. My sister wives already do so much for me that sometimes I feel lazy. I had grown used to taking care of myself—attending to all of my business affairs, my housekeeping, and my child rearing. Now, Janelle does a lot of the accounting for the family. Christine entertains and keeps the kids happy when we are together. Meri gets us all organized for trips. They have taken such an enormous burden off of me. I've had to grow accustomed to having so much taken off my plate. Especially after being on my own for so long, the help and support is welcome. I realize that I don't have to do it all.

At Christmas, I really learned how my sister wives could come through for me. I had been sick leading up to the holidays, and somehow, I had neglected to buy stocking stuffers for my own kids. I didn't realize this until Christmas Eve when the adults were sitting around stuffing stockings. I was horrified. But my sister wives had it covered. I sat there in awe as they produced everything I needed to fill my children's stockings. Now that I've had my first child with Kody, I'm especially excited to see what my sister wives will bring to this experience. They were wonderful throughout my pregnancy, looking out for my needs and lending a hand whenever possible. Meri even has a changing table and baby clothes in her house so she can take care of my baby on her own from time to time. Right away, I could see the perks of having three wonderful women to help me raise not just this child but my three other children.

Of course, there will be struggles down the road. There are days when I'm so mad at one of my sister wives that I want to scream. When this happens, I have to find a quiet moment and talk to God until I arrive at a place where I can calmly talk to my sister wife about what is bothering me. I know that it will be part of my earthly triumph to work out these relationships with these women.

When I think about our relationships and how we develop them, I often think about a muscle. A muscle does not grow and get stronger until it is pushed and tested and sometimes even-torn. When you work out, you are stretching and testing this muscle until it hurts. But when you are done, your muscle is stronger. That's what our relationships are like.

I'm very idealistic about love and marriage. I want it all—the amazing love I share with Kody and the wonderful friendships I know I can have with my sister wives. While I plan never to leave the honeymoon phase of my marriage, I also imagine that I have three women who will ultimately be my best friends forever.

PART THREE

FAMILY

Chapter Nine

MERI

People always ask us if we have a system for running our family, especially for raising our kids. Every time we seem to get some sort of system in place, things change—we move, we change jobs, our kids grow up—and the whole thing reinvents itself.

One of the biggest challenges we faced in figuring out how polygamy would work for us was learning how each wife would maintain her own autonomy while being an important part of the family. When Janelle and Kody first married, the three of us shared a bank account. It wasn't long before we learned that this wasn't an ideal situation. For anyone, money is a tricky subject. Our situation was particularly delicate since we were all new to polygamy.

Our joint bank account was definitely a big part of the struggles we had as a new plural family. When it was just Kody and me, we shared a bank account. All purchases came out of this account, and we paid all the bills from this account. Since it was just the two of us, it was easy to know what we needed and what finances we had available to us. It was comfortable for the two of us to both use the same account. We would talk about what bills needed to be paid and what purchases we wanted to make, either individually or as a household. Although we both had access to the account, and Kody took some part in it, I usually paid the bills each month.

When Janelle came into the family, we added her to the bank account. I don't think any of us really thought about how this would affect us as a whole. Even back then, we would all discuss what the income was each month and what needed to be paid. We worked out a budget for the family, including a grocery budget, a budget for the bills, and our own personal spending budget. We were young, and new in our jobs and careers, so there wasn't usually an abundance of spending money—we'd have to save up if we wanted something special. Kody was in sales, so there were times when he would have a particularly good month and we could put that extra money into either paying down a bill or toward something we had been saving for. While the three of us always discussed where the money would go each month, I was still usually the one who actually paid the bills and divided up the budget. At the time, I saw no problem in this, only to realize later that Janelle felt that I was controlling the finances. In my mind, since we had all discussed it as a family, I was only executing the decision that the three of us had already made. I realize now how detrimental that has been to my relationship with Janelle.

Looking back, I don't remember when we actually decided to get our own bank accounts. I can only assume that one or all of us discovered that having only the one account didn't give each of us, including Kody, our own autonomy, which is very important in a family structure like ours. When we got our own bank accounts, Janelle and I were able to start creating our own autonomy. We didn't have to check in with each other about our spending. We didn't have to be concerned about whether the other would disapprove of a particular purchase. We could handle our financial affairs as we liked and feel that we were individuals who contributed to the same family. Ever since we made this decision, Janelle and I (and subsequently, the other sister wives) have kept our finances separate.

As our family has grown, the way we handle our finances continues to evolve. The most effective way we have found to manage our money thus far is for each of us to take ownership of certain family bills, whether it's the mortgage, the cell phone bill, or a car payment. Even though the bills we pay may not be technically in our own name, we divide them based on each person's income level.

Having a large family as we do, there are often major expenses. There have been times for each of us when we needed help from the family as a group to take care of a certain issue. Usually, if a wife needs help with something, she will talk to Kody about it. Many times, Kody's help is all that's needed. There have been times, however, when he will go to another wife, or wives, to see who is financially able to pool resources and get a particularly tight financial situation taken care of. I remember one time, years ago, when the transmission went out in my car. We all knew it was important to have a working vehicle, so we pulled together to get it taken care of.

Most of his married life, Kody has been a salesman. As most people know, in this line of work, you can have very good months or very bad months. When he has months that are not so good, we all contribute to get the mortgage paid. On the other hand, when he has a good month and ends up with some unexpected cash in his wallet, we can either play catch-up from the bad months, or he has been known to use some of it for something fun, maybe a special trip with a wife and their kids.

Our first commitment is always to the family. However, as the kids have grown older and we've moved into separate households, we've begun to live a little more independently from one another. We look after our own kids, our own homes, and take care of our business in our own way. But this wasn't always the case.

When our oldest kids were young, Janelle worked full-time and Christine worked part-time. So for the majority of the day, I was a stay-at-home mom.

In a lot of areas, I'm a lot more particular about certain things than my sister wives are. I tend to like a little more order and quiet, and I have clear ideas about when and how to discipline the kids. I really struggle when I see the kids being disrespectful to their parents.

It has always been very important to me that our children grow up with a strong sense of respect, for both people and things. When the kids were young, I tried very hard to instill this in them. I wanted them to respect one another by playing nicely together and getting along. I wanted them to respect their parents by being obedient and not talking back when asked to do something. (When I see one of our children do this, it sure gets my Irish up!)

I also think it's necessary for children to respect things. This could be each other's toys, their private space, and yes, this could also be furniture. I'm the type of mom who doesn't allow jumping on furniture. I know I've not always been looked too highly upon by some of my sister wives because this makes me seem too strict, but my furniture has definitely outlived some of theirs! I remember a time, years ago, when Kody was sort of getting after me because he didn't want the kids to feel like they were walking into a museum when they came to my house. I think, however, that he has mellowed somewhat about that opinion, as he has seen my household furniture last longer than that of my sister wives'. Over the years, I have also learned to relax when it comes to the way the kids act in my home. While I still expect them to treat me and my space with respect, and not act like wild animals running through the house, I have become more patient when they do.

Back when I took charge of most of the day care in our family, I was comfortable disciplining all the children, whether Christine's, Janelle's, or mine. Of course, this was easier when the kids were small and their transgressions were fairly innocent. After all, I was the only mother home with anywhere between four and nine kids, depending on the year. If I hadn't felt comfortable disciplining them, the house would have been utter chaos.

Years ago, when we lived in northern Wyoming, when Janelle worked full-time and Christine and I were each working part-time, we adjusted our schedules so that one of us would be home with the kids at all times. This was a particularly good time for our family. We had discovered that it was best for the three of us wives to have our own homes, so we all gained a bit more autonomy and freedom, and could raise our children as we wished. While we all have the same basic goals and expectations for our children, we have a different way of handling our home life and structure. Having our own homes allowed us to interact with our own children comfortably and freely, without having to worry about if another mom was questioning the way something was being handled.

Christine and I had our homes on two and a half acres out in the country, and Janelle had purchased a home in town, about fifteen minutes away. She brought her kids over to our house every day while she worked, so the kids were together all the time. They were one another's best friends. They were constantly building, playing, and creating in our yard. There was so much space to run and play. They created "Kids' Town," which consisted of old blankets, boards, and lumber; anything they could find to make stores, post offices, and houses. They spent many hours in Kids' Town. Since Christine and I lived so close together, we could pop back and forth between our houses with little effort. All the kids knew they were welcome in either home at any time.

It was an unwritten rule that whichever mom was at home with the kids could use her best judgment on the discipline needed for individual situations. We were all pretty comfortable with this, but occasionally, we disagreed. In one instance, I was at work, and Mariah needed to be disciplined, so Christine handled it. When I heard about it later, I was fine with the fact that Christine addressed the problem, but disagreed with the way she punished her. I felt it was inappropriate and a little extreme. We discussed the issue, and while she might disagree with my opinions on discipline, she was very respectful of my feelings.

Mariah is sixteen now, so discipline is somewhat a thing of the past in my house. When the kids were younger, and I had a more active role in their day-to-day parenting, I would choose a punishment to fit the situation. If a child hit another child with a toy, he didn't get to play with that toy anymore. If a child didn't clean up his or her room, he or she didn't get to play outside with the other kids until it was done. I never disciplined the kids if I didn't think they could understand how to correct their behavior.

As the kids have grown older, however, I've taken a backseat in affairs that don't concern my own child directly. I realize that my sister wives and I have different ideas about what is a punishable offense and what isn't. I also realize that the other moms need the space and freedom to do their own thing in their own way.

Of course, I can't always ignore it when the kids do something wrong. As recently as this summer, I felt I had to step in and correct a situation that had gone on too long and needed to change.

Ever since Robyn joined the family, we've been dealing with the typical blended family scenario. Several of Christine and Janelle's kids hadn't been acting like they wanted to accept Robyn as a parent or accept her kids as their siblings. I understand that this is a problem many other families face, yet I know it is still difficult on the kids. Several of the adults began to notice that some of the younger teenage boys were picking on Robyn's little girls. Now this could have just been seen as big brothers' typical treatment of little sisters, but I think if it's bothering the girls, it shouldn't be allowed to continue. It had gone on too long and, in my opinion, nothing was being done to change it.

On a camping trip, things became too aggressive for me to brush aside any longer. A few of the boys were picking on one of the little girls and making her cry. I had enough of it. I got after the kids, telling them they'd better shape up and start treating one another with more respect. I told them that Robyn's kids are their siblings whether they like it or not, and they better start treating them like it. As I was speaking, I noticed that Janelle and Christine just stood there and didn't say anything to back me up. I felt betrayed by their lack of support. I feel strongly that the adults in the family must show a united front to the children, so they know we are all in this together and will support one another's decisions. I think it is very detrimental to let children think they can play one parent against another. But not all the wives feel this way. In fact, later on, Christine told me she thought I was completely out of line for speaking my mind at the moment.

My form of parenting is to take care of things immediately when the transgression is fresh in the children's minds, so they can understand why they are being disciplined. Therefore, I jumped in when I did and talked to the kids about their behavior. Christine would have preferred to wait until later and talk to the kids individually. I'm sure there are pros and cons for each approach—this was just one of those times where we needed to remember to be patient and forgiving with each other. Deep down, we're all working toward the same goal—a happy, healthy, and orderly family.

Obviously, as our children have grown up, one of the major questions in our household has to do with dating. When the kids were little, the adults always said that they would be allowed to date at sixteen. But now that this time has come for many of the kids, we parents have realized that things are not so black and white. We often don't agree, with the children or with one another, on what constitutes a date—is it a group of kids hanging out together? When two kids are hanging out one-on-one? Or just when there's a romantic interest involved? I feel that some of our kids are mature enough to handle themselves on a date, while others might take a few more liberties than I would prefer. We have to figure out a fair way to permit one child to do something another one cannot—something that is difficult for any parent, with children of any age.

As far as dating goes, I stand by my opinion that the kids should be at least sixteen. I don't think dating is necessary any younger than that—it just sets them up for mistakes or heartbreak. Before sixteen, kids don't have the fortitude to deal with emotional and romantic situations. As far as kissing, I think young people should really hold off until they find someone very special, at an older and much more mature age. Kissing can lead to things that teenagers shouldn't get into and definitely don't have the maturity to handle.

I'm in a fortunate position with Mariah when it comes to dating. While she has shown interest in young men, and looks forward to dating in the future, she is committed to remaining in our faith and living our plural lifestyle. With this belief comes her commitment to remaining virtuous and chaste until marriage. She holds high expectations and standards for herself concerning dating, kissing, and intimacy, and she has every intention of living up to them. She plans to finish high school, go on to college, and work toward her dream of becoming a doctor, and has said many times that she does not intend to get married until she's through at least a few years of college. I look forward to seeing her achieve those dreams. I expect she'll have her share of dating and heartbreak before she finds her soul mate, but I also know how stubborn she can be, and that she will live up to her own high standards. Kody and I have talked many times about her passion and commitment to our faith and are very proud of the path she is pursuing. In a lot of ways, I feel as if I have it easier with her choices than some of my sister wives have with their children. I have been absolutely blessed with her, in so many ways!

Mariah and I have always had a special bond. Obviously, we are in a unique position because our household is quite small. On the evenings when Kody isn't around, it's just the two of us. However, Mariah loves being part of our very large family. She often tells me the best thing about polygamy is not being an only child, which she would be if it wasn't for our plural lifestyle. While her commitment to our faith is based on something deeply spiritual, I know that having lots of siblings and many loving parents is definitely a draw to the lifestyle. She doesn't always like being alone and she doesn't like it too quiet, so our family fits her well.

Since we moved to Las Vegas and we're in different homes so far apart from each other, we don't have the constant interaction with the rest of the family that we used to in Utah. Mariah and I definitely have different eating habits than the rest of the family, and now we're able to cater to our tastes more often. When we lived in Utah, I would buy more "kid friendly" foods, knowing that very often, I'd have a child or two extra at mealtimes. That doesn't happen quite as often now, so when the other kids come over and try to find something to eat, it's not too much fun for them.

Mariah and I like to eat a lot of fruits and vegetables, or things that need to be prepared, like salads or fish or chicken.

Since there are only two of us to feed, we don't participate in the big family grocery trips with Janelle and Christine. There's no point in us buying perishable foods in bulk—and I don't have a lot of prepared foods in my cupboards. It even gets frustrating for Kody when he's home that he can't look in the cupboard or the fridge and grab something really quick. What age is it that you turn into your mom? I remember many times looking in my mom's full refrigerator thinking there was nothing to eat. I think Kody feels like that at my house now! I'm pretty particular about what I like, so I haven't always had the best results when I've asked my sister wives to pick up groceries for me. I forget when I give them a list that I need to be very specific. I like my bananas a certain color, and I like certain kinds of lettuce. I forget that their versions of bananas or lettuce can be very different. It usually just makes more sense for me to shop on my own. I tend to make more frequent shopping trips but buy less stuff than my sister wives.

With only one child to feed, I have a lot more freedom and leisure at mealtimes–especially on nights Mariah decides to eat with some of her siblings—which can be frequent. Anytime any of our kids are over at another house at mealtime, it's just a given that the child can stay for the meal. I know all of us moms have an open-door policy for meals, or anything else, when it comes to the children in our family.

Robyn and her kids have joined us for dinner at my house often. There's no rhyme or reason to when this happens, it's just an impromptu event. Sometimes after she's been over for a while, we'll realize that we've lost track of time. Robyn's daughter Aurora really likes to cook and is often the one who asks if they can eat over, and can she be the one to make pancakes for dinner.

These evenings with Robyn have happened with and without Kody present, and I enjoy both ways equally. These bonding moments are important to me, especially now that we all live so separately in Las Vegas. Back in Utah, in the big house, it was easy to interact with one another. There was a little more spontaneity. Now every family gathering needs to be planned in advance. We have family dinner every Friday, but with some of the teenagers having driver's licenses now, and all of them having friends and other activities, there's usually at least a kid or two missing from dinner. In addition, we have lunch together on Sunday afternoons. Whenever we have a family meal, every wife contributes something to help feed the family, unless the meal is a birthday party. In that event, the mother of the birthday boy or girl takes care of the preparations.

Despite the distance between our houses, especially mine, the kids have as much freedom as they like to come and go as they please. Mariah has her driver's license now, and my old car, so she has a lot of freedom to see her siblings pretty much whenever she wants. She spends almost all of her free time with Aspyn, Christine's oldest child, and Madison, Janelle's oldest daughter. Those three girls were all born within three or four months of one another, and have always been very close. Of course, they still have the typical sibling rivalry that most teenage girls deal with, but they always come back to the fact that they are sisters and love one another, and love hanging out with one another. It's been fun watching them grow up so close.

Both Janelle and I have pools at our houses in Las Vegas, but Janelle's pool is more popular than mine because it's a little bigger and within walking distance of the other moms' houses. During the summer, the older kids tended to congregate at Janelle's house, while the little kids came and swam at mine. While I love having the younger children over, the teenagers just don't hang out at my house enough! I miss that. In Utah, my part of the house was central in the home, so it was easy for the kids to just walk through the doorway and be in my house. It was definitely a more quiet part of the house, and the teenagers seemed to congregate there often.

Because I only have one child, my house has always been the quietest of all our homes. Certain kids are drawn to this quiet and, ultimately, to me and what I can offer them. Because I don't have all the extra responsibility and work that comes with having many small children, I can be focused on a child when he or she is in my home. I'm able to offer stability and structure to the kids, whether in the form of calm conversation or a quiet place to do their homework.

Over the years, I've formed an especially close bond with Christine's daughter Ysabel. She and I just sort of click—there's something natural about our relationship. She loves to hang out with me, and when she's being particularly needy, Christine loves for her to hang out with me, too! Ysabel is really precocious and fun, but at age eight, she can be a handful. With five other children, Christine sometimes doesn't have patience for Ysabel. I really like the fact that I can be there to handle Ysabel when Christine is feeling overwhelmed with her. Christine will joke from time to time that Ysabel should come live with me since she loves being at my house so much. Half the time, I'm not sure that she's joking!

In the years since I first met Robyn and her kids, I've also developed a close relationship with her oldest son, Dayton. He and I have a fun, quirky relationship. I think the initial bond for us was that we share a birthday. One of Kody's traditions for all his kids' birthdays is to take that child and his or her mom out for a special birthday "date." This could be anything from shopping for new clothes to going to dinner and a movie. Since Dayton and I share a birthday, he gets a special birthday bonus. He and I will go out and do something, just the two of us. It's something I can do for him that helps to build and cement our relationship.

My bond with Dayton, and all of Robyn's kids, has definitely been an added bonus in the relationship Robyn and I already have. In fact, when I found out Robyn was pregnant, it was easy to quickly form a bond with her unborn child. Early in her pregnancy, I told her that we were going to need to get some baby things at my house, too, since I was sure that her baby would be spending plenty of time there. She agreed, and seemed to like the connection I was forging with her baby. In fact, at her baby shower, she got duplicates of one of the gifts, a baby bouncer seat, and instead of returning one and getting something else she needed, she left one of them at my house to use when her baby is here. I also did a little shopping and got a few little baby boy outfits for him to use while at my house. I was very excited and looked forward to when Solomon would finally be born. Now that he's here, I get together with her often so I can see him and hold him and form a lifetime bond.

I love being part of such a large and dynamic family. There is always something going on with our kids—graduations, sporting events, performances. My sister wives and I are constantly calling or texting one another, keeping everyone aware of all the events in the family. Keeping up with our schedule alone can be a full-time job! While the whole family doesn't usually get to every event, we do our best to make sure there is at least some of the family in attendance.

I try to get to the kids' activities as often as I can, like Hunter's football games. Even though I understand very little about the game, it's fun being there and supporting him from the bleachers. Unfortunately, this last season I only made it to one of Hunter's games. Mariah and some of the other kids, however, attended many more of them. It's so fun to watch the closeness between the kids, and how they support one another in their sporting events and activities. It has especially been exciting to see the evolution of the kids over this first year in Las Vegas, from some of them being so upset and sad about our move, to where they are now, being involved with new friends, teams, and activities.

Unfortunately, with such a large family, one of the problems is that not every event has a large show of family support. At one of Mariah's recent school choir concerts, Kody and I were the only family members in attendance. I wish that more of our family had been there to show their support, but I understand that there's always something going on, whether it's another event, errands to run, or a mom just needing to take a little break and not go anywhere that particular day.

Since we've moved to Las Vegas, our lives have become busier than ever. I really wish the five of us adults had a chance to get together socially more often, but it just doesn't seem possible more than once a month. Oh, we spend a lot of time together when the kids are in school, at least twice weekly, but those times are business and organizational meetings. When we do have the chance to break away, we sometimes have had to make a conscious effort to not talk business, but to just enjoy one another's company. Whenever the adults try to get together, my sister wives have to figure out whether their older kids are willing and available to watch the younger ones. I have to say, though, having just one sixteen-year-old, it's kind of nice to not have to worry about babysitters or homework anymore. Mariah doesn't have to miss out on the experience of babysitting her siblings, though. She is often over at Robyn's house, helping out with her kids, and is happy to do it.

Another thing we try to do fairly often as wives is go out to lunch and reconnect every once in a while. Since we've been in Las Vegas and we live so separately, and our lives have become so busy, meeting like this is a nice break. We do this while the kids are in school, and hopefully while we're away, Kody is also taking the time away from wives and family to renew his own energy. He puts so much out to all of us that it's important for him to have some rejuvenating time as well.

Absolutely too soon, Mariah is going to move out of the house. She'll graduate from high school in 2013, and she is determined and excited to go back to Utah for college. While I'll be sad to see her go, I understand her wanting to return to Utah and get reacquainted with our church community. I'm proud of the commitment she has to her faith, and her desire to return to it, in spite of having to leave her family. She is very excited and looks forward to going back to the friends she left when we moved here a year ago.

I've heard that when people become empty nesters, they have to figure out who they are again. This is kind of how I'm feeling right now. I think in particular, I'll have to figure out what my place is in the family again. It will be a new chapter in my life and my evolution as a sister wife, and it will be interesting to see how it all plays out.

Whenever I talk to Robyn about this, she is so cute. "You still have kids, Meri. You still have kids!" she insists. She's right. I know I do, but it's different from actually having them in my home full-time, and having that constant influence over them.

I'm at a major fork in the road of my life right now, with some major decisions to make, and so far I have no idea which path I will take. On my list of possibilities, these three stand out: I can continue my schooling and work toward my dream of becoming a counselor working with at-risk youth. I have the chance to pursue one of our family businesses by doing some humanitarian work and traveling with friends and family to new places I've never been before.

The third possibility wouldn't be possible if I didn't have sister wives. Over the last couple years, I have been blessed to experience the true love that two sister wives can share. Robyn has shown me this many times, most recently after the birth of her son. Knowing that I have often dreamed of having more children of my own, and knowing that my body is very resistant to the idea, she pulled me aside, and with only the love that a sister wife could give or understand, she offered to carry a child for Kody and me. This would mean becoming a mother again in a way I never would have thought possible.

All three are amazing opportunities that no doubt will fulfill my life in a way I probably never could have imagined. I don't think any of my options are "right" or "wrong" for me, they're just choices with different and amazing outcomes. As I continue to live my life, loving every moment I have with Mariah until she moves on to college and her adult life, I will do the best I can for myself and my family in the role that I am in, and I will work toward writing the newest upcoming chapter in the book of my life. I look forward to my future with hope and anticipation, fully expecting life to bring me all the happiness and fulfillment that I've had in the past, and then some. I have no doubt that it will be a truly amazing chapter!

Chapter Ten

JANELLE

The beauty of living in a polygamous family is that we truly get to embody the principle that "it takes a village to raise a child." Our family is that village. While all of our children have benefited greatly from the different personalities of the five adults who have raised them, it wasn't always easy establishing the rules and guidelines for child rearing. When you have four adults, now five, who all grew up differently, with different freedoms and different household rules, coming to a consensus about what we should tolerate and what we should permit wasn't easy.

In the beginning, when we were just starting our family and Logan was the only child, there was a great deal of conflict over the rules for how the children would behave in the home. While we all did agree on the bigger issues, such as not tolerating it if children are disobedient or disrespectful, it was harder to come to terms about the smaller stuff. Some of the adults did not want Logan to climb on the couches and play with pots and pans in the cupboard. Being an adventurous child, Logan was eager to do these things. I was a permissive mother and allowed him to climb and crawl where he pleased. I wanted him to explore as much as he could as long as he wasn't putting himself in harm's way. Some of the adults didn't agree. So there was a great deal of friction those first two years or so when Logan was learning to crawl and then walk.

Like any parents, we were perhaps a bit too overprotective with the very first baby. Once the other children came along, things began to mellow a bit. My sister wives realized that kids needed to be kids. They would climb and explore and there wasn't all that much we could do to stop them. As our family evolved and we created our own households within the family space, each wife became more and more autonomous. We began to raise our own children the way we wanted to, according to the rules and guidelines we preferred individually. When children visit another mother in that mother's house, they are aware that different rules are in place. For example, in Meri's house, the children know they cannot roughhouse to the same degree that they can in Christine's or mine. One way is not worse than the other, it's just different. The children have learned to respect each mother and act appropriately in her respective household.

But even with difference in rules between the houses, we still all have come to a consensus on the bigger, more universal issues. For example, we all agree on what constitutes disrespect. If any of the children, mine specifically, or those of my sister wives, are acting in a manner that is rude, harmful, or disobedient, any of the mothers is well within her rights to correct that behavior, usually with a scolding. I feel that a transgression that requires more than a scolding is something for the individual mother and Kody to handle. I will alert my sister wife that I have observed a problem but then leave it to her to handle as she needs to. The downside for our teens, especially, is that there is always a parent who could be watching! We joke with the kids that we have eyes and ears everywhere—because often we do. For example, recently I was running errands and observed one of our kids walking on the street quite a distance from home.

Because it seems out of the ordinary, and because we parents communicate frequently, I knew that this teen was usually supposed to be somewhere else at this time. A quick phone call to my sister wife confirmed that it was okay for this teen to be in this unusual place. But if not? Well, then it's accountability time for that child!

When the children were younger, it was easier to cross-discipline them. The rules of behavior are a little more black and white when the transgressions are things such as lying or fighting. As the children have become teenagers, I find it's a little more difficult to interfere with the way in which one of my sister wives manages things. There is a much larger gray area these days regarding what constitutes a transgression. The older kids have developed their own personalities and what one might do to be cheeky, another might do in good fun. One household might have different rules about phones, curfews, television—there are just too many variables at play. We all have strong relationships with our own teens and with each other's teens, but since teens as a whole are more complex, rule and boundary setting is usually left to each particular mom, as she knows her own children best.

Nevertheless, the universal rules apply—none of the adults tolerate blatant disrespect or lying from any of the kids, regardless of age or parentage. When either of these happen, I feel completely comfortable stepping in and asserting myself. I will also intervene when any of our children ignores his or her own mother's instructions. I have no problem acting as a secondary enforcer, so the child knows the mother is to be taken seriously. There are times a particularly contrary kid gets the full force of all adults present ordering him or her to take his or her mother seriously. When this happens, the child knows it's time to shape up!

Compared to Kody and my sister wives, I am a softy. My older children tease me that I never enforce anything I threaten them with. This is mostly true. I feel more comfortable discussing with them what is wrong with their behavior rather than punishing them for it. I have always been a nonconfrontational person, so this is just my parenting style. If not for my sister wives and husband, my children would probably have run wild! The other adults are much quicker than me to carry out their punishments and rarely let bad behavior slide. I credit the way my children have turned out to the fact that my parenting decisions were backed up by Kody, Christine, and Meri, who also provided a structured environment for them and were not afraid to enforce things.

Even when we lived under one roof in the big house in Utah, we still managed separate households (except for the mortgage). Although we discovered long ago that financial autonomy was important to each of us, we do often pass money back and forth between wives to help cover expenses. We all contribute on day-to-day stuff like baby shower gifts and wedding gifts. We also all contribute to larger family expenses such as the cell phone bill.

This is not to say that there wasn't overlap between us while our family was younger. Christine and I especially worked together and helped each other out financially as well as with meals and errands. When we lived in the big house, Christine and I usually did the bulk of our shopping together. It just made sense. Our kids are the same ages and like to eat the same things. On the days I was working, Christine usually made dinner for both my kids and her own. However, on days that I didn't work, I usually cooked for my kids alone. Even when I put food on the table or stock my fridge, my kids are eager to go scavenge in other mothers' fridges and cupboards. It is a universal truth that someone else's food is always more interesting.

The kids have always been free to move from house to house. Obviously in Utah, this was a lot easier than it is now in Las

Vegas. These days there is plenty of walking, driving, and shuttling back and forth. It's a lot of work to keep track of which kids are where, how they got there, how they're getting back, and where they need to be later—everyone is always on the go. But it's comforting to know that our kids are always being supervised by a parent.

There are many evenings, especially on the weekends, when my house is completely quiet because the kids have dispersed to the other houses. Over the summer, my pool was pretty popular with the older kids, while the younger girls always got really excited to have sleepovers at Robyn's. They think it's cool to have a couple of new sisters with different toys and different games. During the school year, Christine and Robyn's houses seem to be where most of the kids want to hang out because they are the easiest places for all the siblings to meet up with each other, as well as with other kids in the neighborhood.

Certain kids often form attachments with mothers other than their own. These can be lifetime bonds, or simply temporary solutions to something a kid is going through during a particular time in his or her life. Currently, Hunter gravitates toward Christine. She has her own way of talking to him and can be more helpful to him during this phase than I can—and for this I am unbelievably grateful.

I'm so glad that my sister wives, as well as Kody, are there with me as we navigate the murky waters of adolescence— especially issues of love and sexuality. For me, the most important lesson to teach my kids is not to get too serious, too fast. The adults constantly back me up and emphasize to our children that serious dating is not at all appropriate in high school. If our kids are to date, we prefer them to go on group dates. With Madison, Logan, and Hunter, I am very blunt in discussing the perils of too much intimacy before they are mature enough to handle it. I never tire of telling them that unexpected babies and STDs could mess up their lives if they're not careful. But boy, do they roll their eyes at me when I get on my soapbox! Fortunately, I'm not in this alone. I have four other adults who will reinforce our vision of morality and help me make sure that my kids conduct themselves as safely as possible.

Despite the complexity of my relationships with my sister wives, the support network we have is unbeatable. In the ideal world, we would all be able to be together as a family as much as possible, but with so many kids running off in so many directions, this is not always possible. I wish that I could attend more school functions than I'm able to. But we have to come up with a "divide and conquer" system. While not every mother can attend every event, no child will ever have a recital, game, play, or graduation without a few members of the family present. So if I can't make it on game day, I know at least one of my sister wives will be there. That is the beauty of our family, especially now that we are able to live out in the open. We can be there for one another without question and without scrutiny. We can finally be the family we always dreamed of being.

Chapter Eleven

CHRISTINE

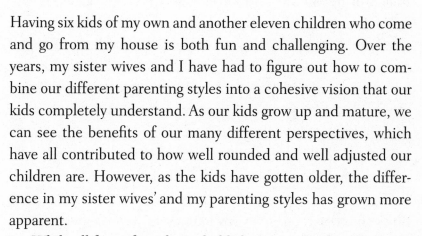

Having six kids of my own and another eleven children who come and go from my house is both fun and challenging. Over the years, my sister wives and I have had to figure out how to combine our different parenting styles into a cohesive vision that our kids completely understand. As our kids grow up and mature, we can see the benefits of our many different perspectives, which have all contributed to how well rounded and well adjusted our children are. However, as the kids have gotten older, the difference in my sister wives' and my parenting styles has grown more apparent.

While all four of our households have more or less the same rules, the enforcement can be quite different! For example, none of us permit jumping on the furniture—but Meri's couches will last her entire lifetime, while Janelle's were broken after a month. Mine get really, really dirty, really, really fast, while Robyn's will remain pristine for a long time.

In the same vein, there's no eating in the living room—in any of our houses. Meri's living room is spotless, without a crumb to be found. Janelle has food spots on her carpet and couches, and I find wrappers shoved in between the couch cushions. Occasionally, I even find plates and forks under my couches. (Robyn is in the "hidden wrapper" camp as well, but not to my extent!)

In many ways, we're lucky that not all of us react the same way to issues with our children. There are times when it seems impossible for me to connect with my kids, so I really lean on my sister wives for help. Meri has a sweet way of engaging Ysabel. She responds to her lovingly and patiently, and Ysabel is sweet back to her and loves Meri. The other day I picked up Ysabel at Meri's house and she told me that Meri was her "bestie." I adore Hunter and he is always welcome in my home. During his difficult adjustment to living in Vegas, he always knew he could come to my house and I would just be there for him. I totally understood why he was feeling troubled—his world was out of his control and he needed Truely time. In the same way, Robyn has been wonderful for Mykelti. She *gets* her, and this has been so important for me because not everyone in the family fully understood her unique outlook. At times, she has really struggled with her identity, and I know it helps her to have family other than Mom to confide in. While all of the wives pitch in to help with the kids however they can, I also go out of my way to interact with my children on a one-to-one basis. I think that individual time is really important in a family as large as ours. We have reading times and time for games—my kids are my favorite hobby.

I regularly organize outings for my group of six, even if they're simple treats. We get ice cream or rent a movie and all watch together in my room. Back in Utah, we went to my mom's house every Sunday. I've tried to keep the tradition of a Sunday expedition now that we're in Las Vegas, but since the traffic here is terrible, we often keep it local—one week we drove out to the desert, and another, we all went bowling downtown. And of course we still do things with the whole family. Since we are away from our church, we worship in our homes instead—we have a family service, followed by a family dinner, which gives us some time to hang out together afterward. In the evenings we usually play games, read, or watch movies—the normal stuff that all families do together.

Since I spend so much time with my kids, I feel that I'm quite tuned into their needs. This allows me to establish realistic punishments on a case-by-case basis. I choose consequences to fit the situation. When Aspyn leaves the car messy, she has to clean it out and vacuum it. When Mykelti wears immodest clothes, I take them away. When Paedon gets bad grades, he doesn't play Xbox. When Gwendlyn picks on Ysabel, she does Ysabel's chores, and when Ysabel is a brat, she can't spend time with me.

One of the major problems I am having these days is with how my older girls, Aspyn and Mykelti, dress. They insist on wearing shirts with low necklines that show an indecent amount of skin. All of the adults agree that even a suggestion of cleavage way oversteps the boundaries of what is appropriate, but the girls keep trying to get away with revealing too much.

If my sister wives and I were to address this problem separately, this is how we would handle it. Meri wouldn't let the girls buy the shirt in the first place. Janelle wouldn't notice the low shirt unless it was unbelievably drastic, but then she'd tell them it was inappropriate. Robyn would give them a lecture on purity, while Meri would want them to express themselves while still remaining within the rules of our family. I just look at them, groan, and ask them to change their shirt or pull it up so it covers more skin. Recently, I've hidden all of the girls' shirts with low necklines—but they keep finding new ones. Argh!

The neckline issue is one that we all agree on as a family; we just have different ways of addressing it. But we don't always see eye-to-eye on other parenting issues. If some of the moms don't agree with how another sister wife is raising her own kids, we may take the liberty of giving her our two cents' worth, but this is rare. However, if I have a problem or a concern with one of my kids and don't know how to handle it, I usually ask another wife's opinion. One of the best things about living in a polygamous marriage is that when I'm unsure about how to approach a situation, chances are one of my sister wives has some great advice— or has lived through the same thing!

One of the things we are all working through together as a family is the dating question. We have a lot of teenagers who are testing the boundaries of what is permissible. As adults, we have to band together to give them constructive guidance so the kids can understand the consequences of taking on too much before they are ready.

As a general rule, before they are sixteen, the kids can hang out with friends and go to dances or movies as long as there is nothing romantic going on. If one of the kids is "crushing" on someone and he or she is not sixteen, they can't go out with that person. Once they are sixteen, the kids can group date. However, they have to wait until they are eighteen for individual couple dates.

As much as we want to strictly enforce these rules, there are always gray areas. When she was fifteen, Mykelti wanted to go to a dance with a friend. She promised that there was nothing romantic at all between this boy and her. They were purely platonic friends. Kody and I agreed to meet him. Then we took her phone from her and read all of her text messages to this boy in order to make sure there was no "crushing" going on. One we were certain that Mykelti and this boy were nothing more than friends, we allowed her to go to the dance.

As it turned out, I had to be out of town for her dance. So I asked Mykelti which of my sister wives she wanted to be her "mom" that night and help her get ready. She chose Robyn. Robyn made sure Mykelti's makeup was done and that she was dressed modestly and her hair was arranged beautifully. (Robyn is great with makeup and hair.) She sent me a photo of Mykelti before the dance, too. It was a cute bonding experience for all of us.

We also let our teenagers have access to social media to keep in touch with their friends, but we monitor their online presence—I think it's brilliant for parenting! It helps all the adults keep tabs on the older kids together, and it's particularly important now that our children are in the public eye. The kids have their own social media accounts on Facebook and Twitter, and we have a family YouTube channel and a family Web page. Aspyn even has her own computer, which she bought after working a summer job.

I ask the kids not to go on blogs about the show, because some people have no conscience online and say whatever they feel—and sometimes it has really hurt our kids. Once a lady was wrecking on Robyn, and Aspyn came to her defense, saying, "She is one of my moms and I love her, and you don't know her. You think you know all of us just from watching us for an hour a week, and you judge us with your small amount of knowledge." I think we all have to learn to deal with controversy in our lives, and the kids are having to learn that now.

Of course, having four households with different house rules does complicate things for the kids. But the pros of this situation far outweigh the cons. I absolutely love that the kids travel from house to house simply because they want to be with one another—or be with other moms. Janelle's boys, Hunter and Garrison, seem to be over at my house a lot, while Ysabel is often at Robyn's or Meri's.

Once the summer ended and pool season came to a close, my house became the house where all the kids hung out. I love hearing them talk all at once and I love joining in their conversations. I think my baby, Truely, is one of the reasons a lot of the kids come over. She's such a funny baby and always up to something crazy that makes everyone laugh. I've always wanted to have the "hangout house" and now I do!

I'm a little stricter when it comes to organized family activities at my house rather than casual hanging out. Whenever the entire family is coming over for a game day or potluck, I make my kids clean the house first. When this happens, they always grumble and tell me they'd rather be hanging out at Janelle's.

Over the years, Janelle and I have developed a symbiotic relationship in which we naturally gravitate toward helping each other out. She works and I take care of the house and kids. In Utah, we either did our shopping together or I'd pick up stuff for her or she'd do the same for me. If I was cooking dinner for her kids and didn't have something, I felt comfortable raiding her fridge or cabinets for what I needed.

Except for our weekly Friday dinners and our Sunday potluck, there has been less overlap between our households since we moved to Vegas. We eat at our own houses most of the time. We tend to congregate more often in groups of two. So many relationships in our family require one-on-one time to properly develop—it's not something that only happens when you're adding a new wife to the family. The kids travel back and forth all the time, but the wives are all busy, so we tend to stick to our own houses and work independently. Our family identity has really changed since the move, and it's sad to think about how we used to interact more often. Now we talk on the phone or have family meetings, but the spontaneity is gone. We have planned meetings, planned lunches. Planned phone calls, blah, blah, blah, boring. I miss all the hanging out, but can't seem to get myself out of my home in the evenings.

Looking into the future, I would like to move back into a house with a sister wife. I miss the communal aspect of our plural lifestyle. Recently, Janelle and I have been looking at houses together. We are a good team. She is practical and can take care of the finance, administration, and bills, while I can take care of cooking, cleaning, and crafts. Our two groups of six children are all close in age and would absolutely love to be under one roof again. The only foreseeable problem we are facing is that we need a house with at least nine bedrooms—a mansion, really! But somehow we will make it work. It helps that both Robyn and Meri like having their own space, and prefer to have their own houses. Some people may think that sister wives are all joined at the hip, but we're a great example of a family in which some people want more closeness and some want more privacy, and we find a way to accommodate everyone.

There will always be changes to our lifestyle. Our family keeps growing and evolving. Logan, our oldest, is already getting college acceptances, and soon Aspyn and Mariah will be, too. Who knows what will happen then? How will we adapt to a slightly emptier nest? I have no idea. But I'm sure whatever happens will be full of surprises, as always.

Chapter Twelve

ROBYN

Since I am a relative newcomer to the Brown family, I do not share as much collective history as the rest of my sister wives do. I've never lived under the same roof with any of them, so I've been spared a lot of the conflicts and growing pains that my sister wives went through as they figured out how to raise their children together and integrate their lives with one another.

Although I lived in my own house when I married Kody, I still became part of the Brown family in every way—I helped out with all the kids and contributed my paycheck to the family to help pay all the bills. This cooperative living was new for me; as a single working mom, it was usually up to me to make things work financially. Money was tight, but knowing that we had one another's backs was wonderful.

Since moving to Nevada, things have changed a lot for us and made us more of a team. We all had to contribute to the expenses to relocate our family, which was difficult for each of us. But now that we have a television show, we are essentially working together as a family on a daily basis and we are a team financially. We split all of our money evenly and help each other out. This has unified us and evened out any sense of financial inferiority or instability any of us may have had previously. We are all equal.

Obviously, in addition to bringing a greater sense of financial equality between us, the show has been beneficial in allowing us to openly attend all of the children's school activities. The adults know that all the kids love to have any, if not all, of the parents at their recitals, performances, sporting events, and assemblies. If I could, I would go to every school event! Unfortunately, with so many children, this simply isn't possible. Each week, all the moms and the kids let the family know about what school events are happening and we try to figure out a way for the most parents to attend the most events. When my son Dayton graduated from elementary school, I invited all the parents. To my surprise and delight, they all came. Christine got there first and texted the rest of us, letting us know where the assembly was and that she was saving seats. When we all sat down and Dayton saw us, he starting waving. Sitting in the audience, I was overwhelmed with pride in both my son and my family.

One of the benefits of being in a plural family is that when I simply cannot attend one of my kids' events, I know that my sister wives and Kody will give my children support I would have had I been there. Sadly, Kody and I had to be out of town when Dayton was a in a school play. I knew how upset Dayton would be if no one from the family was there—he was so excited to be in the production. When I asked the other moms to support him, I was thrilled that Christine and Meri were able to go. Meri even filmed the performance so I could watch it later. Dayton was over the moon that his other moms were there. And I was so happy to be able to watch the play when I returned from my trip.

Being part of the Brown family is exciting and surprising for the kids and me. I love that my kids have a ton of siblings around all the time. The other kids are often at my house searching for

food. This is a common habit of all Brown kids—looking for
snacks in the other houses. I specifically save leftovers for such
raids. I always try to have ice cream and Popsicles in my freezer
so the kids won't waste money on the ice cream truck. Even if
there isn't ice cream, there's usually something worth foraging
for in my cabinets since food has a tendency to last longer at my
house. My girls and I don't eat a lot. I struggle to have an appe-
tite. But Breanna and I are both hypoglycemic, which means we
always need to have emergency snacks on hand so that if we experience a blood sugar crash, we can survive.

Aside from our Friday night dinner and Sunday potluck, we
don't get together as a family for meals and we don't grocery shop
together unless it's an impromptu event. We will coordinate
our big family meals for holidays and birthdays by communicating who is responsible for bringing what. Birthdays are usually hosted by the mother of the child whose birthday it is. That
mom will cook what she or her child likes best. However, sometimes kids will request a dish from one of the other mothers' rep-
ertoires. Last year Janelle's son Gabe requested Meri's mashed
potatoes and gravy for his birthday, and Meri was happy to provide them. I'll feel pretty special when the kids request one of my
recipes for their birthday meal.

Our kids spend as much time together as possible. The only
rules I impose on this is that visiting children can't interfere
with my children's homework, nor can my kids go out until their
homework or chores are complete. Other than that, as long as I
know where my children are planning to hang out and how they
are getting there and back, I'm happy to have them be with their
siblings whenever they want.

The younger girls tend to congregate at my house. Kody calls
the five younger girls (not including Truely, who's still a baby)
"The Pixies," so my house is sort of the "Pixie House." The girls
range from six to ten years old and they all play together often.

They play dolls, house, do crafts, and anything that fits into their fantasies. They also love sleeping over at my house. I get bombarded every weekend for sleepovers and I get complaints if at least one sleepover doesn't happen per week!

The only time I will assert myself with children who are not my own is when there aren't other parents around. Without the other moms present, I'm comfortable correcting other children's behavior and enforcing my own rules. However, I tend not to do any child rearing with the other children, especially if other moms are present. I don't feel that it is my place to interfere with how someone else raises her children. For this reason, I haven't had a lot of child-rearing conflicts with my sister wives.

While I'm usually comfortable with one of my sister wives helping to parent my children, when we're all together or at another mom's house, I try to make sure I am the one who keeps my kids in line, so another mom doesn't feel like she has to take charge. I feel like I am slacking if I don't take care of things myself and attend to my own children, so I'm very aware of what my kids are doing when we are in another house. When I'm not there and my kids are visiting alone, I encourage the other moms to inform me if my kids are behaving in a way that I should correct.

Despite the fact that all of our parenting styles are different, each sister wife has the best interest of the kids at heart. I'm more prone to talking things out. I want to learn about the kids' feelings and try to understand why they are acting out in a certain way before punishing them for their behavior. I know that I am overprotective and overly gentle. I stand up for the underdog. For example, Mykelti, Christine's second oldest daughter, is a very unique girl. She doesn't fit in very well with the three older teen girls. She is creative and independent, so she gets razzed a lot. I have a tendency to stand up for her and see the best in her. She will do something great someday with her out-of-the-box thinking.

I don't tolerate bullying and harassing from any of the kids.

Even minor teasing is off-limits. I want all the children to be nice to one another always. For this reason, I prefer a calmer more peaceful home environment. I try to bring a sense of respect to every family gathering and every situation in which I'm dealing with a group of kids. I expect the kids to be responsible and considerate, so I try to lead by example.

I ran into a few issues with my position as a parent with some of the older kids when I first came into the family. I don't think they were ready to accept me as a mom—it was strange for them to all of a sudden have someone new parent them without any history. We have had some issues with some of the kids because of this; I think every blended family deals with similar problems. I thought, at first, that my sister wives would just insist that their kids look at me as a mom, but I've realized that it is up to me to claim that role. I have actually had to reach out to the kids and build a relationship with them independent of their biological moms. Respect is earned, not demanded—my parental relationships are getting better and better with time, but it's still a work in progress.

I think opening the lines of communication about our children is important to our growth as a family. We have a lot of kids who are all going through different stages in life. It's essential to stay on top of their development and difficulties. Since my children are the youngest of our brood, I haven't yet had to deal with the question of teen dating. That will happen too soon, I'm afraid. My son, Dayton, is hitting puberty and is almost as tall as me! However, I will happily give my input as to what I think is appropriate so that we can set some family ground rules and our kids will all be on the same page as to what is allowed. I have life experiences that I can share with the kids to help them make informed decisions and I don't mind doing so. Nevertheless, I feel that it is ultimately up to Kody and the other moms to enforce the rules for their specific children.

My children are so blessed to have all these mommies and the best daddy ever. Kody is such a great father, even though he is stretched so thin. He makes time count! I know my kids have felt the lack of having a good daddy in their life. I remember long before I ever met Kody, my kids would ask when they were going to get their new dad. I think Dayton, especially, has benefited so much from having a guy around. Kody is so patient with him and loves to spend time letting him rattle on about his latest fascination. My girls, Aurora and Breanna, adore Kody as well. Daddy's kisses and hugs are welcome and wanted. He is so cute with them. It makes me love him that much more. It really is true that the way to a divorced mom's heart is through her kids!

I'm sure sometimes the kids get sick of having so many adults commenting on their lives. But mostly the kids adore having five adults who love them—not to mention a lot of brothers and sisters who do as well. Our children are never alone and this gives them a strong identity and a permanent sense of place. These kids will never lack in support and love. Of course, being part of such a large family is as demanding of them as it is of the adults. The most difficult thing for our children is that they never get to be selfish and cannot put their individual needs in front of their siblings'. I know my kids have had to adjust to sharing with more brothers and sisters. My girls now have several other sisters to incorporate in their play, whether they like it or not. Recently one of the other pixies needed a chapter book to read and my daughter Aurora has several. I asked her to share with her sister. Aurora struggled at first with lending out her book, so I had to point out that we are a family and we share and we help each other out. This family is always a team. It can be a challenge to them to always remember that. Then again, it can be a challenge for the adults as well. But we are getting there.

PART FOUR

CELEBRITY

Chapter Thirteen

MERI

I have always been very private about my polygamous lifestyle. Growing up, I went to a school run by our church, which meant that during my childhood, I had few friends outside my faith. As I grew older, I met more people from outside my religious community, but I was still quite guarded about my family's beliefs. I kept my friends at a distance and didn't open up to them about my father and his wives. I always offered to hang out with my friends at their houses and never invited them home with me.

I kept my beliefs a secret because I wanted to be accepted as a "normal" person, whatever that means. Essentially, I didn't want to be stereotyped. I wanted my friends to accept me for me and not reject me based on my faith.

After I married Kody—who is so naturally outgoing—I still kept my lifestyle to myself. It wasn't something I was comfortable sharing. I worried about how my friends would react when I came out to them as a polygamist. I didn't want to invite unneeded scrutiny. I didn't want to be judged. Since polygamy is not just frowned upon, but denigrated, you never know how someone will react when you tell him or her the truth about your beliefs. You never know when you are going to lose a close friend. For years it just seemed better to stay quiet.

After Janelle and Christine joined the family, we would explain each other away as sisters, or as Kody's sisters. It was always so uncomfortable to lie to my friends. Lying is not part of our faith, nor part of my own moral compass, so to feel as if I had to lie, or at least not tell the full truth, was quite difficult for me.

Unfortunately, we felt that keeping the truth hidden about our family was a necessity. Growing up, I heard many stories of fathers in polygamous families who were sent to jail for their beliefs. I heard about children taken from their families and wives sent to live in different states, in an attempt to preserve the spiritual family structure. Once Kody, Janelle, Christine, and I had kids, we didn't want to do anything that would jeopardize our family. We needed to stay together even if it meant hiding the truth about our lifestyle. Nothing was going to split up our family.

A lot of polygamists prefer to live in smaller, closed communities where nearly all the residents are of the same faith. These communities, which are actually fully functional towns, have businesses and stores, and some even have their own zip codes. There is a school and of course a church. Since everyone shares the same beliefs, it's simple to be open about the polygamous lifestyle.

I've never lived in a community like this, either before or since my marriage. For years we hid in plain sight. It is a testament to how—and I hesitate to use the word—*normal* we are, that not many people suspected there was anything different about our family. We worked. We had friends outside our faith. We participated in civic life. For many years, I tried not to technically "lie." I always tried to answer questions in a way that might make me feel not so guilty, but I was still not being honest. This is a hard game to play. You always have to remember who you told what to. It was always difficult for me to deny the truth about myself and my family. Lying about our lifestyle transformed something we believed to be beautiful and sacred into a dirty little secret, something that people might think I was ashamed of. It was exhausting and frustrating.

The year before we decided to participate in *Sister Wives,* a very good friend of mine, with whom I'd worked for a few years, invited me to his wedding. Scott and his fiancée, who were both LDS, were planning to get married in the Mormon temple. In the LDS faith, the temple is a very sacred place, and the only people who enter are devout members of the faith who follow specific guidelines. Since we are not members of the LDS faith, the temple would be off-limits to us. Kody and I would be unable to witness the ceremony.

Since there is considerable overlap of beliefs between my faith and the LDS faith, Scott always assumed that I was a conventional Mormon, and I never bothered to correct him. Naturally, when he invited Kody and me to the wedding, he never imagined he was breaking a fundamental rule of his faith. Kody had been suggesting for quite some time that I open up to Scott about my family and my faith. I was too concerned about losing a friend, so I just wasn't willing to do it. I told Kody I was just going to make an excuse to Scott and say we couldn't make it. Because Scott and I had been such good friends, Kody felt that Scott deserved to know the truth about why we couldn't attend his wedding, not just blowing him off saying we couldn't make it. He was very emphatic now that we needed to tell Scott the truth.

Kody and I arranged a dinner with Scott and his fiancée. I was really nervous. I had no idea how Scott would react. My worries were twofold. On the one hand, I was worried that Scott would reject me for my beliefs, and on the other, I was worried he would be angry that I'd lied to him for so long.

Over dinner, Kody managed to steer the conversation around to how Scott and his wife met. After he heard their story, he shared ours. Kody told them that when he returned from his LDS mission, he fell in love with a woman whose father had five wives. It took Scott a moment to realize that Kody was talking about *me*. Once Scott caught on, we explained that we had embraced my father's faith as well and were practicing members of the faith, with a much larger family than Scott had ever imagined.

When Kody and I were done speaking, Scott was silent for a moment. Then he began to apologize. He apologized for putting me in such a difficult position by inviting me to a wedding I couldn't attend. He apologized if at any time during our friendship he might have made a remark about polygamy that was insensitive. I thought it said so much about Scott's character to be the one apologizing, when I was the one who really needed to apologize to him for not being honest about who I really was.

Even though we couldn't attend the ceremony in the temple, we still went to Scott's wedding reception. I felt honored that Scott had considered me such a close friend that he would invite us to his temple wedding, and I was so relieved that our friendship was still intact after opening up about my family and our beliefs. Since then, Scott and his wife have met and accepted our entire family, and even once appeared briefly on an episode of *Sister Wives*.

Incidents like this were frequent in our lives. I think our entire family was starting to feel that in order to live our lives to the fullest, we needed to make some changes.

Kody is a dreamer, which is one of the qualities I love about him. He tends to reach for the stars and in so doing, can come up with some pretty amazing ideas. During our twenty-two years together, I've learned to listen to his ideas and realize that while some are great and we can make them happen, some can be less than realistic, and we need to allow them to fall by the wayside.

Kody had talked for more than a year about wanting to do something to show that plural marriage can be *so* much more than what was usually portrayed in the media—but it took some time to figure out just how to do that. When we met Tim Gibbons, our producer, and the idea of doing a television program was introduced to us, Kody got on board with the idea long before I did. When he told me he was interested in doing a reality program about our family, I just shook my head and let it slide. After all, I assumed this was another one of those plans that he would eventually drop.

I was wrong. Kody did not drop the idea. In fact, he became more and more drawn to it. Soon his discussions of doing a television program went from abstract to serious. Kody felt that he was truly called to the cause.

As our family has grown, so has the time we've devoted to family discussions—decisions about money, schooling, and our living situation. As Kody realized more and more the importance of doing the show, and the calling he felt to it, these discussions became more frequent and more urgent. We spent hours running through the pros and cons of going public.

Initially, I resisted the urge to come out as a polygamist. I have never been ashamed of my lifestyle—in fact, quite the opposite. However, I didn't want to be judged for it. Most of all, I didn't want our children to suffer because their parents had revealed themselves to the world. Kody explained that this show was important and necessary. We needed to step out from the shadow of Warren Jeffs and the FLDS, who for too long had been the face of polygamy. We needed to disassociate ourselves from the negative connotations of polygamy—child brides, sexual abuse, and religious oppression. We wanted to show America that we aren't really that different from anyone else. Most important, we needed to pave the way for a better and more tolerant future for our children. This, Kody explained, would be the purpose of the show.

Although Kody felt called to do this show, it took me a while to come to terms with going public after having guarded my privacy my whole life. It took many conversations with Kody and the family before I started to feel comfortable with the vision he had in mind for us. It also took many conversations with God; I knew we would be looked down upon for taking our family public, so I needed a strong indication from God that this was what He wanted for us.

Deep down in my heart, I knew Kody was right. Secrecy breeds evil and unhappiness, and for too long, that is the only thing about polygamy that had been portrayed in the media. While I was nervous about all the repercussions of taking our story public, I knew that I needed to support my husband. Ultimately, I wanted the world to know that what most people think of when they think of polygamy has no place in our family. We are a great family, with the normal disagreements and laughter, heartbreak and happiness of any American household. I guess I started to believe that our story was worth telling. I contemplated long and hard over my decision. Eventually, I also felt the call to go public with our story; it just took a little longer than it did Kody. In the end, I agreed to do the show and prayed for the best.

Once we committed to being on television, I became incredibly nervous. I was concerned about how people I had known for years would feel about me. I was worried that the children would be ostracized by their friends. I knew from the beginning that there would be those from our own faith who would support us in the message we were sending, but even more who just wouldn't understand. I was worried that we'd be made into pariahs.

It wasn't until I told my daughter, Mariah, about the show that I realized how important it could be to her future. I explained to her that our primary intention in doing a reality program and opening up about our faith was so people would be more accepting of our beliefs. After I told her this, Mariah said, "Mom, you say that you are doing this so that we all can be open. But I've never been secretive about my faith. I've always been open with my friends." While this was true, most of Mariah's friends at the time were kids from our own faith, so there really was no risk involved, she was still young, and her world was the church and the church school. I had to point out to her how easy things can be when you rarely associate with anyone outside the faith. Mariah is so confident in herself and her faith that it never occurred to her that there could be a whole world out there opposed to her lifestyle and her religion.

Unlike many of our other children, until that time, Mariah hadn't had a lot of experience with friends outside our religious community. She is a very spiritual young woman and dedicated to our church. She's naturally drawn to people who share her morals, standards, and beliefs—which usually means they share her faith as well. She hasn't yet had the misfortune to suffer on account of others' intolerance, and she doesn't know what it is like in the real world—the cruelty and fear that might temper her enjoyment of life. As her mom, I want to protect her from having to experience these things, yet I don't want her believing that our religious community is the only place that she could be safe being who she is. There's a big world out there and I want her to enjoy it without having to lie about her beliefs.

At the young age of sixteen, Mariah has already expressed a devotion and desire to live the principle of plural marriage and remain in our faith. While I know she's a teenager and may or may not actually follow through with this plan, I hope that when the time does come, she will be confident enough in herself and her relationship with God to be able to come to her own decision. I believe in order for her to make this decision she needs to feel comfortable in the society of those outside our faith. She needs to have a wealth of experiences before choosing the path for her adult life. I want the world to be a safe and tolerant place for her.

When we thought about doing *Sister Wives,* I knew that if all went well, the show would make it possible for Mariah to live openly, without feeling judgment or oppression. She might live as she pleased in public without fears of ostracism or rejection. She would be given freedom and opportunities that I wouldn't have dreamed of when I was her age.

The first day the cameras showed up at our house was strange and uncomfortable. I was completely unprepared when I came up the stairs into my living room and saw a cameraman there. I had no idea how to behave. I felt awkward trying to act as if nothing out of the ordinary was happening. I'm not the actor in our family—that would be Christine. When the cameras first started rolling, it was difficult to behave naturally as the crew instructed.

It took all of us a while to adjust to having our lives filmed. Whenever the cameras were around, the kids, who are excitable enough, became hyper. Family dinner, our Friday tradition, went from mild chaos to an all-out zoo. I did my best not to modify my behavior for the cameras, but it's hard not to be aware of how you look when people are filming you every hour of the day. One of the things that I'm very particular about is not letting myself be seen without my makeup. When Tim Gibbons, our producer, wants to film an early morning episode, I'm up an hour beforehand getting ready, doing my hair and makeup. This way I can truly look like a "TV star," waking up in the morning with perfect hair and makeup. This doesn't really have anything to do with being vain—I think of it as protecting the world from a good scare!

Eventually, I grew used to having my life filmed. Often what they're filming seems really uninteresting—which I guess is good in a way. After all, we are a pretty normal family that does normal things. I'm happy to show the world our everyday reality and defuse the myth that there is anything weird or inappropriate about our lifestyle.

However, every once in a while, private issues crop up that we don't want to share with the public. In general, the crew is respectful of our wishes to keep some issues off camera. They will generously leave the room when we need privacy to deal with a particularly difficult matter. Of course, the production staff does push and probe us. They want drama, after all. Since I'm a black-and-white person, I don't hold back, even on TV. It's not in my nature to sugarcoat things, even for a national audience. On TV as in real life, I can only be my honest self. The Meri you see on the show is the person you'd meet face-to-face.

I don't think any of us realized what a strange experience it was going to be discussing our lives in front of a producer. The "couch sessions," in which we talk about issues and problems, were a real wake-up call for our family. We had to learn to think before we spoke. At first, when the producer would ask us questions about a particular situation, each of us would answer as if he or she was alone with the camera, and not sitting on the couch with the rest of the family. Often one of us would inadvertently throw a sister wife or Kody under the bus, publicly airing a grievance that would have been better dealt with in private.

These couch sessions turned into a public form of therapy. Issues that might have remained dormant were quickly brought out into the open. One of the things that the producers were eager to dig into was my relationship with Robyn. They latched onto my struggle with Kody and Robyn's courtship and exploited it into a major story line. I can't really blame them. After all, this was, in reality, what I was dealing with at the time.

When they first started filming the show, Robyn and I were going through an unbelievably difficult period. After getting the ball rolling between Robyn and Kody, I had just stepped back in order to allow them to have the time, space, and freedom to get to know each other better. I was at a low point, feeling unwanted and unloved. I know I wasn't being as kind or welcoming as I could have been.

Despite this struggle, Robyn and I knew that we wanted a good relationship with each other. The couch sessions helped to bring our issues into the open, and we began to address them on the show and behind the scenes. The beauty of it is that over the course of that first season, Robyn and I developed a wonderful relationship. Fans of the show can see just how close we've become. Whenever they stop us in public, we almost always get some sort of comment about our relationship.

Watching how we began to overcome our initial struggles and differences and became close friends is both rewarding and satisfying to me. It's also important, for it shows the audience that something that seems dysfunctional at the start actually works when you give it some time. The success of Robyn's and my friendship is essential to understanding the beauty of the sister wife relationship. Like Robyn and myself, our family is constantly evolving for the better. The show brought that process to light, both for us and for the audience.

When I look back on the first season, I'm thrilled by our family's evolution. I love our collective strength and the maturity that has developed. Of course, there are still some moments during that first season that, while interesting to the public, I have chosen not to watch, one of those being the honeymoon episode. Kody, Robyn, and I have made such progress in our relationships that I worry seeing them in such a romantic setting might set me back a few steps. I'm sure I'll watch it one day when I trust myself with my emotions a little more. The wedding reception episode, however, is my favorite moment of the show! When I watch it, I'm overwhelmed by the love and joy I see on the screen.

While I certainly benefited from being given an additional forum to work through some of my personal issues, when the show began to air, our family suffered both individually and as a whole. Right before the first episode premiered, an article appeared in a Utah newspaper about our family and the upcoming reality show.

I was working at a rehabilitation center for troubled youth at the time. Again, I was in a situation where I felt it was best to keep my family and religious beliefs to myself. When one of my coworkers read the article, she was shocked, not because of my beliefs, but because I hadn't been open with her. "I had no idea you had this lifestyle," she said. The fact that I was a sister wife didn't bother her at all. I felt relieved that she now knew, and still accepted me as her friend—and I hoped my employers would be just as accepting.

I had discussed my lifestyle and our family being on a reality show with my immediate supervisor, who had subsequently discussed the situation with upper management. No one seemed concerned for six weeks—but the day after the series premiere of *Sister Wives,* the Lehi City police department sent out a press release that they had been investigating our family. The next time I went to work, upper management called me into the office and fired me. I was devastated. All I wanted to do was help troubled kids, and I was being terminated because my employer was afraid of somehow being involved with this police investigation. They said to me, "Meri, what happens if the police show up here at the facility?" Management told me that they were not firing me because I was a polygamist, but because they were concerned the investigation would bring unwanted attention to the facility and the children housed there. Suddenly, I'd gone from being a private person to being a public figure, and a controversial one at that.

Losing my job was the most difficult thing I suffered as an individual once the show aired. It made me question whether or not our family had really done the right thing in going public. At my core, I knew it was right for us, but suddenly having to deal with losing a job that I loved and was very good at made me angry.

Our kids started to come home from school on almost a daily basis with new questions or comments from classmates about their dad being prosecuted. I remember one time the kids told us that a neighbor boy had told them that he had heard Kody was going to jail. Sometimes when our kids were playing outside or walking home from school, they would see a police car on the road and get nervous, wondering why he was driving down our quiet street. Bombarded by these questions and fears, we felt it would be the best thing for us to move away and try to bring some sort of peace back to our children.

While the move was difficult on the parents, it was terrible for our children, who were being separated from their friends and the only life some of them had ever known. I can't blame them for thinking that we had done something terrible to them by forcing them to move. It's difficult for them, especially the older children who had deeper roots in Utah, to appreciate the positive impact of the show, when all they can see is that because of the show, they had to leave their friends behind.

I know that when the dust settles, the children will begin to understand how important this show is. Already, their lives are so much different from what they used to be. They attend large public schools in Las Vegas, where they are open about being brothers and sisters. They acknowledge one another in public in a way that was nearly impossible for my generation. They have many new friends, from all different faiths and backgrounds, who accept them and do not judge them. The show has demystified our lifestyle and allowed the kids to be kids.

The show has opened up new avenues to the adults as well. The veil of secrecy behind which we had been hiding has been completely obliterated. I feel such a sense of relief that I can finally be open with so many of my oldest friends. Last summer, I was able to introduce Robyn and Christine and many of our kids to my dear friends who ran the trophy engraving shop in Wyoming, where I worked all those years ago.

It's wonderful to be open in public. We no longer worry about what it looks like when Kody and four wives go to a restaurant together. We are proud to be a family. It's also great to get so much positive feedback and support from complete strangers on the street. However, I don't think I'll ever get used to people coming up to me and telling me that I'm their favorite wife. It just doesn't make any sense to me.

Although we are recognized around our neighborhood in Las Vegas, it completely took me by surprise when people in New York and Chicago approached me on the street on our publicity tours. I almost have to laugh whenever anyone uses words like "celebrity" or "famous" to describe me. I'm neither of these. I'm just a mom and a wife who happens to be on TV. I'm just me.

Doing the show has allowed us to see some amazing cities and meet amazing people, all while causing us some of the worst stress we've ever had. We've visited Times Square, Hollywood, and Chicago. We've met Ellen and Rosie, and the four oldest kids even got to meet Oprah with us. I was so excited when I had the opportunity to introduce myself to Matthew McConaughey, only to have Robyn and Christine ruin the moment by acting like giddy fourteen-year-olds around him! I've been a huge fan of Matthew's for years. Although it's not true, I often tease Kody that Matthew is the reason I let him grow his hair long.

When we travel for the show, we get booked in some fantastic high-rise hotels with awesome views. One of my favorites was looking out over Central Park in New York City. I know this sounds like such a wonderful experience, but the downside is that when we're on these trips, we are usually going, going, going, to the point that we don't get to enjoy the room or the view at all! On most occasions, we're up at the crack of dawn, running all day, only to come back to the room too late at night to do anything but fall into bed and try to be ready for another day. Sometimes, because of the tight schedule we're usually up against, our emotions can really get the best of us. One thing we have all had to learn to do through this is to get phenomenally better at patience, kindness, and forgiveness.

In addition to the ups and downs of travel, there's also the negative publicity we've had to deal with. Once you become a public figure, you lay yourself open to that. I know that there will always be someone who has something unpleasant to say about my marriage, my hair, my weight, or any number of other things—it just comes with the territory. My way of dealing with it all? I choose to ignore the polls and commentary on the Internet about our show or family members. I have more important things to do with my time!

In many ways the show has unified us. When we travel together, we are a tightly knit group. We don't let anyone breach our boundaries because together we exhibit strength in numbers, which is the backbone of our family unity. Being open in public has only reinforced that. Our strength in the face of public scrutiny is what makes us special. It's what makes our show positive and important for us and for our children.

Chapter Fourteen

JANELLE

Once I converted to the fundamentalist faith, I realized how easy it is to be a Mormon in Utah. Even though Mormons only make up 50 percent of the population there, I've read that an estimated 80 percent of the lawmakers in Utah are LDS. When I married Kody, I was no longer a member of this dominant group. I was fringe. I was an outsider.

In polygamous communities, there is a great deal of cultural fear. People my mother's age regularly shared personal experiences of having their families split up by the government. These stories had a great impact on me, and I became very worried about someone finding out I wasn't like them. I kept my head down. I rarely discussed my family and private life with outsiders or colleagues.

The *Sister Wives* television show, which changed my way of thinking and brought me into the public as a polygamist, was a slow and gradual evolution. Of course, I was nervous about exposing our family. However, the more we talked about the show the more enthusiastic I became.

While we were filming the first season, I got swept away by

the project. It was exciting. A new energy had been injected into our lives. I was so caught up in filming and all the coordination that comes with mobilizing our entire family to move as a unit to various shooting locations that I didn't give much thought to the fact that the show would eventually be seen by, we hoped, millions of people.

I wasn't nearly as afraid while we were filming the first episodes as when we finished. Suddenly, the show was done. They were editing it. It was going to be on the air. There was no turning back.

The summer before the show aired, I was stressed out beyond belief. Many of our peers had parents who were put in jail during the governmental raids of the 1950s. There had been no recent raids on our communities. The raid in Texas was on an FLDS community, a completely different group from ours. But the stories in our cultural memory suddenly took on a new life for me, especially at three o'clock in the morning when I was lying awake in bed.

I couldn't put my worries aside, even going so far as to seek counseling at one point. This annoyed Kody. Before the network announced our show as part of the fall line-up, Kody told me, "You need to think more positively. This is a positive thing for our family, our faith, and the world." I tried, but I'm more of a realist than my husband.

After my concerns about my family, one of my gravest worries was about my job. I'm completely career minded and working means a great deal to me. To make things more difficult, I worked for the government in a job I loved. If there was any employer who would fire me, I was sure it would be this one.

In Utah, everyone always assumes that you are Mormon, especially if you don't smoke or drink. Since I was raised LDS, it was easy for me to be a chameleon at work. I could talk the talk and walk the walk. I wanted to seem Mormon enough not to draw attention to myself. This was easy since I understood conversations about aspects of conventional Mormonism, such as "visiting teaching lessons," and "wards." While I understood this sort of office chatter, I always stayed on the periphery of these conversations.

Sometimes I tried to throw my coworkers off the scent about my religion and disassociate myself from all forms of Mormonism, LDS, or fundamentalist. I started drinking coffee, something Mormons are prohibited from doing. I sorely needed caffeine at work when I had five kids under the age of six! I'm not sure what my coworkers thought when I started drinking coffee, but they never once asked me about my faith.

Before we traveled to Los Angeles to introduce *Sister Wives* to the public, I still hadn't come clean to my coworkers and my superiors about either my lifestyle or the show. I was nervous about having this conversation. Kody told me not to bother. He urged me to let them discover the show on their own. We had no idea it would become front-page news in Utah.

It's not in my nature to share more than necessary, but I felt that the ethical thing to do was to tell my supervisors the truth about the show and my family. I figured if I was to be terminated, I wanted to allow them to do it discreetly before *Sister Wives* began.

I waited to tell them until the day before we left for California to announce the show to the Television Critics Association. After all, I wanted to keep my paycheck as long as possible. It took a moment for my bosses to get over their initial shock—not only was I a polygamist (because I didn't look like one), I was going to be a public one. After we finished talking, they went to the Human Resources Department to see what should be done about my situation. The people in Human Resources were very open-minded. They told me that as long as I never mentioned my job, what I did in my private life was up to me—even if my private life was going to be on television.

I was thrilled with this outcome, since I had been expecting the worst. Contrary to conventional belief, Utah is quite diverse: My coworkers were a mixed bag of races, religions, and sexual persuasions. When I came out as a polygamist, I was delighted to discover no discrimination in my workplace. As I see it, God loves everyone equally regardless of lifestyle, religion, or race. I was glad to find that my superiors seemed to hold the same opinion.

Despite everything, I was still unbelievably nervous when it came time to announce the show. At the Television Critics Association, we waited backstage while they played a clip from the show. After the clip finished, we were ushered onto the stage in front of a room full of critics. There was no going back.

Immediately, a journalist from the *Deseret News* in Salt Lake raised his hand. "Aren't you worried that you're going to go to jail like Tom Green?" he asked.

My two greatest fears coalesced into this one question. First off, the world thought we were criminals who would be sent to jail. And even worse, we were being compared to Tom Green, an independent Mormon fundamentalist who had been jailed for statutory rape after marrying his thirteen-year-old stepdaughter. But ending these sorts of repulsive comparisons was reason enough to go public with our story. Although this was precisely the reaction I most feared, it also told me that what we were doing was necessary and right.

At first we were all taken aback by the journalist's question. After a few seconds we gathered our composure. "We're nothing like Tom Green," we told the reporter. "That's why we feel we have to tell our story."

After the show was announced to the public, TLC began to air promotional clips on a pretty steady rotation. Naturally, they wanted to draw as much attention as possible to the show, so they chose the sound bite where we briefly discuss sex. We had decided to address this issue head-on and quickly get it out of the way, so we could move on with the rest of the show. But the brevity of the clip made it seem as if we were going to come out with something really juicy and salacious! Of course, the truth was just the opposite, but the promotional ads started to create serious waves in our community. To TLC's credit, when we told them it was making our day-to-day lives more difficult, the network changed the clip immediately. We felt so honored that our requests were taken seriously.

When our church community saw the preview they understandably became upset. Many hadn't been thrilled with our decision to do the program in the first place, and now they were worried that we were going to be sensational and improper. Once they discovered that we intended to film Robyn's wedding reception, some members became even more concerned.

The wedding ceremony in either a fundamentalist faith or in the LDS church is sacred and private. No one outside the faith is allowed to witness this ceremony. It's never discussed. The promo for our program aired shortly after the HBO series *Big Love* had filmed a sensationalized version of the temple ceremony. So when our church community got wind of the fact that cameras were going to be at Robyn's reception, they were alarmed. Eventually we managed to convince our fellow church members that we had absolutely no intention of sensationalizing either our lives or Robyn's wedding. Our plans were only to film the reception and show our collective happiness at Robyn and Kody's nuptials.

Soon after the show aired, I noticed that we had already had an impact on the way the world perceived polygamy. I was flipping through the TV directory looking for something to watch when I came across a show called *The Lost Boys*. The brief blurb described the show as being about "Members of the Warren Jeffs FLDS sect." This was progress. A few months earlier, I'm sure that the description would have been about "polygamist Mormons." But now people were beginning to differentiate between the sects, and understand that we had nothing to do with Warren Jeffs and his abusive practices.

Although the show helped the public to understand our faith a little better, it also led to misunderstandings within our own family. I don't think anyone in the family was prepared for the emotional toll of our "couch sessions." Suddenly, what was supposed to be a lighthearted look at our fairly normal family turned into an investigation into our emotional scars and private struggles.

When we set out to do the show, we imagined it would something like *19 Kids and Counting*, which follows the daily life of the Duggar family. This show is light and frothy with an emphasis on family. We thought our show would touch on the sweeter side of our life and never probe beneath the surface. We were totally unprepared for the reality of confronting our issues in front of the TV cameras.

Initially, these sessions were intended to allow us to recap events on the show, but we found that we were unearthing emotional hurts that we had skimmed over to keep the peace. There are times when we don't watch our words and put our feet in our mouths.

When Kody let slip that he had selected Robyn's wedding dress himself, even after Meri, Christine, and I had taken her shopping as an important bonding experience, Christine was devastated and walked off set. The show has to fit into an hour of television, so the necessary edits made it look as if she returned immediately. The truth is that she didn't come back for three days. We were a mess after that session. It took a while for us to heal, but we are stronger for it.

Robyn is usually instrumental after a particularly difficult couch session. We really give her mediation skills a workout. Sometimes she starts the healing process right there on the set, not letting us leave the room until we've settled whatever troubling topic our producer has asked us to talk about.

Misunderstandings within the family are not the only problems that have cropped up in light of the show. The way the media perceives and treats us has been something of a surprise. Educated, intelligent people have made strange and off-color comments that have not just shocked us but offended us on a very deep level.

When people hear the word *polygamy*, their minds often jump to salacious conclusions. For some reason, many intelligent Americans cannot differentiate between a healthy, polygamous family and a man cheating on his wife—or even a harem! On our first publicity tour, during a preinterview for a nationwide talk show, the interviewer asked us some unbelievably personal questions about our intimate lives. We were asked about whether we compare our sex lives behind Kody's back and if we could comment on the difference in the intimate natures of each marriage. Our publicist jumped to our defense and demanded to know what woman in her right mind would answer the sort of questions we were being asked. Our publicist pointed out to this interviewer that she certainly would not ask the same questions of other reality show stars—not even on the most sexually provocative shows. We were so grateful to her for stepping in, because I'd been left speechless at the interviewer's complete lack of tact!

Of course, I understand that people want to know about our

private lives. Everyone always wants to find something scandalous in something pure. I hope that the show has firmly established that we are involved in four separate marriages and we keep our personal intimacy as private as possible. None of us want to know what goes on between Kody and another wife in their private time.

Of course, the show has made it more and more difficult to remain unaware of how Kody and my sister wives behave in their individual marriages. In fact, since much of our lives is televised, I'm confronted with a great deal more of these other marriages than I was comfortable with in the past. I have to do my best to fight the impulse to compare my marriage to those of my sister wives. There are certain things on the show that I'm not comfortable watching, such as Kody's intimate moments with another wife. (Robyn's honeymoon certainly falls into this category.) I'm not a jealous person, but I just don't care to see how Kody and Meri or Kody and Christine interact. This has always been one of my personal boundaries. It's the problem of apples once again. This show has made it necessary for me to find the security and strength to not want apples simply because someone else has them. If I want a pear, I'm going to ask Kody for a pear.

Even though interviewers often tried to dig for something juicy and salacious in our private lives—for exactly the kind of thing we never discuss—I enjoyed myself on our publicity tours. I love watching the behind-the-scenes efforts that go into our show. I enjoy learning about marketing and media and the business side of the reality TV business. Since I handle the contracts for our family, I've acquired a lot of knowledge about the financial side of the entertainment industry—something I'd never imagined I'd come into contact with.

I have always loved to travel. With six kids and a sixty-hour work week, for most of my adult life, travel was put on the back burner. Once we began to promote the show, we were able to visit major cities as a single-family unit—something I never imagined would be possible. This freedom to be ourselves is unbelievably liberating. It's almost a luxurious feeling to go around in public as a family without fear or shame. Before this, only Meri, the legal wife, would go with Kody to any official functions. But now we go as a group. Whether or not people condone what we do, everyone acknowledges me as Kody's wife. The simple peace of not having to remember to use my "cover story" has been a relief. I love being able to express my pride in being Kody's wife without fear or anxiety.

Naturally, the show has provided me opportunities to experience other things I would never have been able to, such as taking the kids on a camping trip to Big Bear, renting a cabin in the mountains at Christmas, and going snowmobiling. But there was a damper put on things very quickly. The Lehi City police department announced on the day our show premiered that they had been investigating our family since we introduced the show at the Television Critics Association.

We introduced the show in September and by November it was clear that we were going to have to leave Utah or risk the safety of our family. We decided not to tell anyone—not our friends, coworkers, or even the producers of our show. We didn't want to make a big deal out of our decision and we wanted to protect our children while we figured out our next move. In fact, we told TLC only shortly before we moved. We obviously had a production schedule lined up and this was a huge change in those plans. We really weren't sure they would continue the show, but we had made our minds up as a family that it was the best thing for us to move out of state.

We felt it would be best for our kids if we put some distance between our family and some of the emotional stressors in Utah. It was a heartbreaking moment when I explained to my children that we were moving to Las Vegas. Madison, my oldest daughter, began screaming, "You can't make me go! I'm going to run away." Hunter, my second boy, just sobbed and sobbed. My oldest, Logan, was stoic. He simply squared his shoulders and said, "Okay, let's do what we need to do."

It was devastating having to separate the kids from their friends and take them out of the big house. But it is my belief that everything happens for a reason. The move to Las Vegas has been instrumental in exposing our children to a more diverse culture. This is an important step to help them decide what faith they will follow when the time comes. For some of my children, I think polygamy would be an appropriate choice. For others, I'm not yet sure. I know that most of them are eager to return to Utah. The morality evident in Utah still appeals to many of the kids, and for this I am grateful.

However, exposure to different types of people and different lifestyles will help my kids make better and more informed choices. I'm sure when they are off at college—and the only thing I ask of them is that they go to college—they will look back on their time in Las Vegas not as a trial but as a period of intense and important growth.

I have also seen some wonderful benefits for myself in the move to Las Vegas. Since we are living openly for the first time ever, I no longer have to censor myself and hide my home life from new acquaintances. I have a much richer and diverse social life in Las Vegas than I ever had in Utah or Wyoming. I no longer worry about people coming into our houses. In fact, I am always excited to welcome our neighbors—something I never imagined I'd be able to do back in Utah.

Despite that fact that for the first time in my life I have a much larger circle of friends, leaving Utah has also been a period of personal upheaval for me. Obviously, my government job didn't travel with me. I struggled through a period of unemployment, which was difficult for a gal who had always defined herself by her career. I did a lot of behind-the-scenes family administration, but it didn't take the place of a full-time job.

Kody and I had both more and less time together. Less time, as Kody was spread thin between four separate homes, and more time because we were all looking for work. Kody and I really struggled with each other. When I'm yanked out of familiar surroundings, I often begin to question my place in the world and in the family. Not having a job for the first time in ages really shook me. I have always identified myself as a career woman, and now, for the first time in my life, I was a stay-at-home mom.

Shortly after we arrived in Vegas, I found myself in the throes of a full-fledged identity crisis. I was miserable and I took that misery out on others, especially Kody. I was on a veritable fault-finding mission. He couldn't do anything right. Every issue I'd ever had with him in the past began to bubble up and boil over. Our whole lives were in upheaval. I knew that in order for things to settle down both physically and emotionally, Kody and I would have to clean house, throw out the trash that had accumulated in our marriage, and move forward. But first, we had to hit rock bottom.

I didn't know who I was anymore, and Kody was as lost as I was. We had to work to an even deeper level of honesty with each other. It was a very hard time. At one point, we even looked at each other, and for the first time in our lives said, "Are we sure we married the right people?"

For two weeks, we could barely be civil to each other. Being alone was unpleasant to say the least. I was in a foul, dark place, and Kody, instead of trying to lift my spirits, sunk down with me. There was no sweetness and little love. After eighteen years of marriage, we were being downright, brutally mean to each other.

I knew that this couldn't continue. I didn't want our relationship to disintegrate. So one day, I decided to say something caring to Kody. He immediately responded with something loving in return. And that was all it took.

Once the doors of communication between us were open once more, I realized that I needed to be honest with myself about what I wanted from Kody and be able to ask for it. I also realized I had begun to take Kody for granted and I needed to give as much as I was receiving from him. Upon moving to Vegas, I had rebuilt the wall around myself and I was unwilling to show any vulnerability. I told Kody that I was going to let him in once more, but that he had to tread carefully. Kody appreciated my honesty and my willingness to open up to him. He in return communicated to me, perhaps more honestly than he had in years, some things he needed me to give to him—more love and affection. As I've always said, our relationship keeps evolving. Where we are now is not where we will be in six months, but it always seems to get deeper and richer as time passes.

When we decided to do the show, we never imagined we would be "TV personalities." I'm still shocked when someone recognizes me while I'm jogging down the street at six in the morning in my sweats and sunglasses. Fame was never on our radar. Our intention was simply to educate people and increase tolerance for our way of life.

I hope that we'll be able to do the show until it runs its natural course on television, until we're bored with it or people are bored with us. It's fun. But when it's over, it's over. Soon our kids will be in college, and after that, we'll be busy with grandkids. We'll look back on the show as something fun we did at one point in our lives.

I hope that when it is over, we'll have changed people's perceptions of polygamy. I do not understand how people cannot be tolerant in this day and age. Once I left mainstream religion and joined an alternative faith, I grew to respect all people who re-commit to their beliefs on a daily basis despite public opinion. I hope our show is a testimony to that strength. It will be our leg-acy. Now that I've experienced what a difference it makes to talk about my faith openly, I can't imagine not encouraging others to do the same.

Chapter Fifteen

CHRISTINE

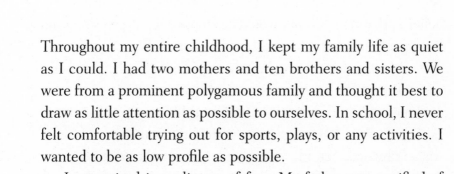

Throughout my entire childhood, I kept my family life as quiet as I could. I had two mothers and ten brothers and sisters. We were from a prominent polygamous family and thought it best to draw as little attention as possible to ourselves. In school, I never felt comfortable trying out for sports, plays, or any activities. I wanted to be as low profile as possible.

I was raised in a climate of fear. My father was terrified of our family being split up. When he was eight years old, his life was turned on end when his parents were arrested for bigamy and thrown in jail. They were released after a single night. (This is common, especially in the case of female polygamists, who are usually sent home to look after the children.)

My grandparents initially thought their arrest was symbolic and that they would have no more trouble with the law. Not long after their release, however, they got word that the authorities were pursuing them once again. My grandfather fled and went into hiding. All of my grandmothers separated from one another and took their children to live in different states or in far-off corners of the same state. This separation meant that my father was permanently cut off from his siblings. For years, he had no idea where the rest of his family was.

My dad was drafted into the Vietnam War when he was nineteen. He was frustrated that he had to serve a country whose laws denied his family fundamental civil rights and caused them to live in fear. Even though my father had been separated from my grandfather, my grandfather still believed in the importance of serving America, and he urged my dad to go and be proud of who he was. Although my grandfather and his family lived a lifetime of fear, he still realized that fear leads to secrecy, and secrecy leads to abuse of power. He advocated for harsher punishment for underage marriages and abusive relationships. He believed that these crimes would be stopped if polygamists could live openly instead of in secrecy. As my grandfather saw it, secret, closed societies were directly responsible for the abuses for which the FLDS has become, sadly, infamous.

Openness in theory is a lot different from openness in practice. And while I knew that my grandfather's theory and belief was entirely correct, incorporating it into my everyday existence took a lot of time.

I'm a very bubbly and outgoing person. As I grew older, I realized that I wasn't always going to be possible for me to hide my family or lifestyle from everyone I met. It's just not in my nature to mistrust the outside world as I'd been raised to do. I look on the bright side of absolutely everything. I expect the best from people. Maybe for this reason, I often let it slip, both accidentally and on purpose, that I was polygamous.

Kody often says that because of my sweet nature, people have no choice but to accept me for who I am. This is honestly the best compliment he could pay me. Perhaps because of my blind trust in the good in humankind—or maybe because I'm a chatterbox!—people began to learn about my family. Their reactions were far more positive than I'd been raised to expect.

Soon after I married Kody and moved to Powell, Wyoming, I got a wonderful job assisting a curator at a local museum. My boss was a fantastic woman. Since we worked in a tiny office— it was just the two of us—I knew we'd be spending an inordinate amount of time together.

The first day at work, my boss asked me about my family and my home life. I told her about my husband, Kody, and his two sisters, Meri and Janelle, who lived with us. I explained that Meri and I both had daughters and Janelle had a son. I said that my sisters-in-law lived with us for financial reasons. I acknowledged that our living situation was a little unusual, but that we made it work.

When the day was over I got in my car to drive home. I turned on the ignition but couldn't bring myself to leave the parking lot. I hated myself for having lied to my boss on my first day of work. I turned off the car and marched back into the museum.

My boss was surprised to see me back so soon.

"I lied to you," I said. "I'm sorry. Kody is my husband. Meri and Janelle are my sister wives. Together we have three children and I will always refer to these children as my children since we are one family."

My boss smiled. "I had a feeling this was the case," she said. She never judged me, and she never said a single bad word about my family or my lifestyle.

Eventually, I opened up to another woman at the museum. She was actually a little envious of the family support I had with my sister wives. She imagined it would have been useful for her when she raised her children. She'd also been wondering how I could accomplish so much at home and at work while raising children.

After I'd been married to Kody for several years, I was asked to represent our faith in a nonprofit organization, Principle Voices. Except for the FLDS, each sect of Mormon fundamentalism has two members on the board of Principle Voices. The mission of this organization is to educate others about polygamous families and culture. The group's goal is to empower both polygamous individuals and families, as well as to provide crisis referrals and response to those in the lifestyle.

Principle Voices is the public face of polygamy. It exists to deal with issues not just inside our culture but outside it as well. The group handles inquiries from the media—requests for interviews and assistance with research. It also interacts with the government on a regular basis, mostly through the governmental organization Safety Net.

Since I am pretty talkative by nature and was getting comfortable talking about my faith, I was often asked to do interviews with the media. Principle Voices gave us extensive media training about how to field questions regarding abuse, sex, and our faith. We were taught how to skim the surface of the question, give a truthful answer without going into too much detail. I learned how to deflect questions from my faith and sex and turn the subject to my family. The underlying principle was to convey our message about our considered and mature choices to live a plural life and to help people to understand our community. As a member of Principle Voices, I spent two years educating people about polygamy. I spoke at colleges and on the news. I became the spokesperson for our faith and I loved it.

After I had been on Principle Voices for a few years, I started to think that openness about our lifestyle might lead to more freedom. This realization coincided with an offer from a television journalist who was looking for a polygamist family to interview. Principle Voices thought my family would be a perfect fit for the show. The adults held jobs. The kids were healthy and happy. There were no underage or incestuous marriages. We were a fairly average, stable, all-American family.

I wouldn't have volunteered my family for this experience

without first discussing it with Kody, Meri, and Janelle. Eventually, the four adults and our six eldest children flew to New York for the interview. Although we were running a risk appearing as a family in front of television cameras, the risk was tempered by the fact that the journalist didn't have an actual television program on the air yet. He was using our story as a demo or a promo that wouldn't be shown to the public. Although we spoke openly on the show, the whole event seemed somewhat secretive and private, which was a great relief.

Appearing on this program led us to a paradigm shift as a family. Suddenly, hiding out seemed less intimidating and less possible than it had before. The production crew mentioned doing a documentary show with our family, and even though we refused, it started to make us think about the possibilities of telling our story publicly. Although I was beginning to feel that it was time to take a public stand, I didn't think a documentary was the right format. While I didn't mind speaking to reporters about my own personal choices, opening our family to the world was really scary. I had legitimate concerns. I didn't want Kody to be taken away as my grandfather had been, and I didn't want anyone in the family to lose his or her job on account of our beliefs.

Even though we turned down the offer to do an in-depth documentary, the family continued to discuss several possibilities for going public with our story. While none of these appealed to me, Kody began to realize that living openly was something he was being called to do. He wanted to help educate people about our lifestyle and to create more understanding and tolerant world for our children.

Any documentary maker or television producer who wants to explore polygamy first goes to Principle Voices. For years, the woman who leads the organization has been fielding requests for families willing to tell their story to the public. There are very few families and individuals who want to participate in anything that could endanger, harm, or just expose their family, especially when it comes to a large-scale media event. I was one of these people. I didn't mind the interviews that I participated in alone, but involving my whole family had until now remained out of the question.

I was approached a few times about telling our family story. One day I told Kody how often I was asked about coming out as a family and sharing our life with the public. "Why didn't you tell me about any of these requests?" Kody asked. Aside from the interview we had done in New York and a brief segment on the BBC that wasn't shown in America, it hadn't occurred to me to tell Kody about the requests for interviews. While Kody was very supportive of my role in Principle Voices and shared my views about opening up our society, I didn't imagine that the rest of our family would want to go public.

"The next time you're approached about telling our family story, let me know," Kody said.

By coincidence, I'd been contacted through Principle Voices by an independent producer, Tim Gibbons, who was looking to do a reality show about a polygamous family. Kody liked the sound of the project and made an appointment to meet Tim in person. Shortly after their initial meeting, Tim came to our home to talk with us about his ideas.

We were immediately impressed with Tim's vision for the show. He had observed the ways in which polygamists were often ridiculed, and felt a reality show could go a long way to changing that. He thought that if he portrayed our family as honestly and openly as possible and showed how essentially normal we are, that people might begin to understand that there's not a whole lot of difference between most polygamists and the rest of the world.

Tim assured us that the crew would be small and unobtrusive. He said that they would respect our wishes whenever we needed to deal with something off camera. Tim's attitude and outlook were so honorable that he put the entire family at ease. Naturally, there was a great deal of debate. But in the end, we agreed to participate.

It was the right time to tell our story. Warren Jeffs was on trial and the news was flooded with pictures of him marrying under-age girls. We needed to provide a counterpoint to that image. We wanted to let the world know that we in no way condone forcible or underage marriage. We do not support any organization that permits a woman to be taken from her family and reassigned to another husband. These things are not acceptable and they have no place in our world.

When we consented to the program, we told our children that they should start letting all of their friends know about our family. (Their closest friends already knew about our lifestyle.) My oldest, Aspyn, was really stressed about telling some of her friends, but when she did, it went really smoothly and everyone was very accepting of her. However, Madison, Janelle's oldest girl, had a totally different experience. One of the girls in her class asked her if being a polygamist meant that her father molested her, she had to marry her uncle, and couldn't wear the color red. Madison was disgusted and horrified. But she was able to demystify the truth about her family and make her friend understand that her home life is pretty normal and completely healthy.

Once Aspyn, Madison, and most of our other children had told all their friends about our family, they could bring larger groups of friends over to the big house, which they loved. The kids thought it was really cool that they could lead their friends through the house and show them the different apartments and introduce them to their different moms.

While the kids were saddled with the problem of opening up to their friends, the adults had a different problem. We had to tell our families, who naturally worried that we might inadver-

tently expose them on the show. My family agreed with my decision to go public, but they were concerned that I'd bring them
into it. They weren't ready to be outed. I had to work hard to convince them that I would never dishonor their wishes and mention their names or show them on television. As we prepared to
do the show, we took steps to hide certain identifying details so
that our family would stay out of sight, both on television and online. While we knew that it would be impossible to protect our
families' privacy entirely, we attempted to do our best and hoped
that the media would respect our boundaries.

While my family quickly came to terms with my participation
in a reality show, I'm afraid that most of the members of our faith
were disappointed with our decision to go public. The plural lifestyle is considered sacred and many people feel that exhibiting it
for the public is like casting pearls before swine. While I am sad
to have angered and disappointed so many in my faith, I do not
understand how they can tolerate the fact that the world thinks
we all marry off our fourteen-year-old girls to older men. I cannot understand why they are content to live in secrecy and fear.
If I had to upset them to make the world a better place, this was
a risk that I was willing to take.

When filming began, it was really strange. It took me a while
to get used to having a camera around. Tim would interview us
about day-to-day activities and I'd be at a loss to see why anyone would be interested in hearing about groceries, teacher con-
ferences, and cleaning. It was difficult to know how to behave
with the camera rolling. It seems trivial to be concerned about
superficial things, but if I knew the crew was showing up for an
early morning shoot, I worried about how I would look without
makeup. Should I do my hair? Can I let them see me in my paja-
mas? These were totally new concerns in my life.

Suddenly, even the most basic things got a lot more complicated. Life was pleasantly chaotic before, but the show

really added a new dimension. I worried about my kids' outfits and their uncombed hair. I realized that some of their rooms might look unacceptable to a television audience. I had to re-paint them and buy new bedding and bunk beds. I also real-ized how dirty the house was. I'm a pretty aggressive cleaner, but with five kids and another on the way (I was pregnant with Tru-ely when we started shooting) cleaning became a job in itself. Of course there was an upside to all of this—there's nothing wrong with a cleaner house and nicer furniture.

Once we started filming, I had to learn how to be comfort-able talking about my lifestyle in front of the camera. My previ-ous media training had instructed me to get the message across about the choices that I made in accepting polygamy. But now I could be as open as I wanted about my own marriage. It was a strange transition to share everything from my love for Kody and my children to struggles both inside the family and outside it.

Of course, frankness isn't always advisable. While I was com-fortable talking honestly on camera for *Sister Wives,* I was hesi-tant to be as open during our press tours. By the time we began publicity for the show, I had learned to trust that Tim and his staff would be honorable when they edited our footage. They didn't change what we said for dramatic effect and they always conveyed the meaning of our confessions exactly as we wished. However, I didn't have as much faith in the outside media. I quickly discovered that they would edit our answers to suit their purposes and tease something salacious from our story.

We made a point of addressing sex in the first episode of our show. We wanted to get it over with so there would be no fur-ther questions. We were willing to do this, especially because we were certain that nothing improper would be made of our words. However, during our press junkets the media always ham-mered away at the sex question. We had to find countless ways of deflecting it. Journalists always wanted to know why we were willing to talk about sex, however briefly, on the show, but not in an interview. It was hard for us to tell a person directly that we didn't entirely trust his or her intentions. Other television shows and news programs have their own agenda, making it impossible to guarantee we came across as we wished. This made talking about sex completely out of the question.

The media tours were insane. Nearly every day, we had a packed schedule of back-to-back interviews. We got tired, but we still had to remain on guard. We needed to watch every word that came out of our mouths, so that nothing could be twisted or misconstrued. We wanted the proper messages to get out there—the positive ones that pertained to love and family. Despite our best intentions, from time to time we said the wrong things and had to do a little damage control. But this can only be expected. We are five normal, middle-American adults with little or no experience in the ways of the media.

On the media tours, it was our goal to get across the basic facts about our family and debunk the myths that most people ascribe to us. No matter what a journalist asked, we tried to steer the conversation back to something positive. We wanted to come across true to our natures and beliefs, as well as strong, independent adults who've come to our faith of our own volition. We wanted to make it perfectly clear that our children make their own choices—they don't have to live polygamy if they don't want to. And most of all, we wanted to convey the stability and love of our family.

During our press junket in New York, we appeared on *Nightline*. I thought the interview, conducted by Dan Harris, had gone really well and I was pleased. The night it aired, Kody and I were in our hotel room. (It was completely surreal sitting in a fancy hotel in New York City, watching myself on TV and thinking about all the people in the same city watching the same show at the same time!) When the announcer introduced our segment it was clear that she thought we were ridiculous. Her tone of voice and facial expressions made her contempt for us clear. She didn't hide the fact that she thought our lifestyle was wrong.

After this less than reassuring introduction, they cut away to the interview, which included wonderful clips of our children. When they returned to the announcer, she was smiling. Her whole demeanor had changed. We'd clearly made an impact. I remember thinking about the millions of people who'd just watched the same thing and how we might have influenced their thinking for the better.

Not all journalists are as kind or considerate as Dan Harris was. After a particularly long day of interviews on that first press tour, I had reached my breaking point. One of the journalists had been pretty brutal to me. He asked me too many questions about whether or not our lifestyle or the show was fair to our kids. He kept trying to get me to admit that I had ruined my children's lives by putting them on TV and exposing them to the public. He really wanted to force my hand and get me to slip up and say something he could use against me.

When the interview was over, I nearly broke down. "I need my people," I said. Then my family gathered around me. We joined together in prayer. I drew strength from them and was able to refocus. On tour, we really help to strengthen one another and build one another up, which is phenomenal. Since we are able to travel openly as a family—something I hope all polygamous families will one day do—we can be there for every moment. We rely on one another for support during the tough questions and the long days. We are one another's safety net. We are stronger than I'd ever imagined.

However, traveling as a family is not always easy. Being on the road as a group of five adults is a completely new and unexpected experience, and it has made our differences more obvious. We've learned that we really have to meet each individual's needs and that as a group we have to listen to one another and accommodate one another. We have had to learn how to express in a polite and constructive manner when someone's behavior is bothering us.

I learned, for example, that sometimes I really embarrass Janelle. I can be kind of goofy in public. I thought it was all in good fun, but I realize that my actions are embarrassing to her and I feel terrible about this. What she thinks is acceptable in public is far different from what I think is acceptable. We've had to come to a place where we can both have fun and be relaxed, while respecting each other's boundaries.

Now that we've figured out how to address our various needs and differences, I've grown to love doing things together. I feel a force of power when we are in a big group. We really are dynamic. Sometimes I feel as if we could conquer the world!

Part of this empowering feeling comes from the freedom of being open as a family. I know that our decision has made us stronger adults and more secure, not just in our individual marriages but as a single-family unit. I'm especially happy for our kids—no longer do they have to duck awkward questions from curious schoolmates or strangers who wonder how so many siblings could be so close in age. Even now in their Las Vegas public school, they are proud to call one another brother and sister. Now Janelle's kids confidently introduce me to their friends as "one of my moms."

I think openness has brought them closer together. They are a tightly knit group, unafraid to hang out together during school. They are happy to draw attention to themselves and their special relationships. Their classmates refer to them as the Cullens— the vampire clan in the *Twilight* books. Together, they are a force to be reckoned with.

Our decision to live openly has allowed our entire family to come into our own. I love meeting all the kids' friends, and I absolutely love taking my sister wives' children places and introducing them as my kids. I enjoy being open about being married to Kody and we do many things as a married couple, and he can openly say we are all his wives. It's fun going places together and being recognized. People meet us and talk about how we have changed their minds and their perspective on families and relationships. I feel humbled and overjoyed at the response we receive about our family, people grateful that we opened up our lives so they could see this plural family choice.

Chapter Sixteen

ROBYN

When I was in middle school and high school, none of my friends knew about my religion. I am the child of my father's second wife, which meant that legally and publicly he couldn't acknowledge me as his daughter. This was difficult at times and hard for a young child to understand. I remember when I was about ten being at a park with my father and my mother and my full biological siblings. When my father noticed one of his work colleagues approaching us, he walked away from my mother, my brothers and sisters, and me. He acted as if he didn't know us. Of course, I knew that he was doing this out of necessity. He wanted to protect us and his job. Nevertheless, it hurt me terribly.

My mother would usually explain the presence of her sister wife by saying she was my father's sister or his wife from a previous marriage who had remained amicable with the family. For the most part, people bought it.

I went to a sizable public school. There were students from different races and religions, but the majority were LDS. My fellow students, and even my teachers, often made disparaging comments about polygamists. They said we were backward and wrong. They openly made fun of the polygamous families that lived in our county. The majority of these families were FLDS. They were openly recognizable because of their extremely modest dress and the women's strange, old-fashioned hairstyles. My family was nothing like these families, but I was distraught by these comments all the same.

I spent my childhood and teenage years terrified someone might uncover the truth about my family. I had few friends, and those I did have didn't seem to question or care about the strange unexplained things in my life. I kept most friends at a distance so they wouldn't start wondering about my family and asking questions.

I did have one friend in the mainstream. Her name was Danielle Scott, and she was LDS. Danielle and I were best friends for many years. When we were in high school, I decided to tell her about my family. I was tired of hiding things from her.

When I told Danielle that my family was polygamous and that I had two mothers, she began to cry. "I thought you guys were the perfect LDS family," she said.

She was understandably confused. Most LDS followers condemn fundamentalism and polygamy. Suddenly Danielle felt as if she didn't know me at all and what she'd just learned about me made me morally wrong.

When Danielle got over her initial shock, she began coming over to my house regularly. She realized that I was just me and my "perfect LDS family" was not all that different than what she'd previously imagined it to be. She grew close to my mom and came to understand that the differences between our faiths were not a big deal. We could be friends regardless of our beliefs.

Over time, Danielle and I agreed to disagree about religion. This was a healthy development. We do try and stay away from the hot-button topics with each other. But this agreement has led to a completely open, safe, and sweet relationship between us in which we can tell each other anything and everything.

I had been the first wife in my first marriage. Although we were in the same church that I am in now, we never got to the stage in which we considered taking on a second wife. My husband and I believed the principle, but things were too rocky between us to consider a plural marriage. This meant that during our marriage, we never really had to worry about how we looked to outsiders. We were a young couple with three young children. It was easy to "pass" as Mormon.

When I started dating Kody, however, hiding the truth about my faith became trickier. When people asked me about the man I was dating, I didn't know what to tell them. Since Kody often visited me in St. George, acquaintances were aware that he had children. When they asked me how many, I never knew how to answer. Should I say one, because that's how many he has from his only legal marriage? Or should I admit the truth and say thirteen? I can only imagine what the reaction would have been if I said the man I was dating had thirteen kids!

Hiding who I am is not in my nature. It's always bothered me that I have to lie about my beliefs, family, and lifestyle. It has made me feel like a second-class citizen. In general, I'm quite honest and outgoing. I have no problems talking about what is going on in my heart or in my head. Sadly, hiding my religion has been an unfortunate necessity. As much as I wished that I didn't have to lie about my faith, I wasn't entirely prepared to be as open as Kody hinted I might have to be if I chose to marry him.

When Kody first told me that he and my potential future sister wives were going to be on a television program, I dismissed it as a pipe dream. I didn't question him or challenge him, but I remember thinking, *Yeah right, you're going to be on TV!*

As our courtship progressed toward engagement, I realized that the television show, which had seemed like a huge fantasy, was in fact a reality. If I married Kody, I would be signing on for this show.

This gave me pause. It was very scary for me. I had been through an incredibly difficult marriage and divorce. I had suffered through some tough times, and now I was being asked to open up about my lifestyle, perhaps endangering my kids and myself in the process. I didn't want this. I didn't need this. I just wanted to live a quiet and tranquil life, happy with God and my family. But I loved Kody and his family too much. I had asked God for a testimony that Kody and I shared a destiny, and I received that testimony. I wasn't turning back.

While Kody and I were courting, I went through a period where I turned to God and asked Him, "You seriously want me to be on a TV show? This is what you want for me?" It just seemed preposterous. I know that God guides my life, but He seemed to be leading me down a strange and dangerous path.

I did consider not marrying Kody because of the show. I was searching for stability and simplicity. Instead, I was hurtling toward a big, scary unknown. I remember being very concerned about the consequences we might face when our show aired. It would hit me some days how crazy going public was. Did I really want this kind of attention? Ultimately, my overwhelming love for Kody, for his family, and my testimony that I belonged in his family won out. If our destiny meant being on a reality show, I was willing.

When my sister wives told their families about the show, most of their relatives came to terms with the decision to go public as long as their own families were not dragged into the spotlight. My family, however, was horrified by my decision. They could not accept or understand this choice. They found it morally wrong and personally dangerous.

Some of my family members think that the plural lifestyle is too sacred to show to the public. They believe that what I'm doing is sacrilegious. I'm muddying the waters of something celestial and sensationalizing it.

In addition to condemning the morality of my decision, most of my family was horrified by the attention they worried the show would bring to them. I fear that when I made my choice to participate in *Sister Wives,* I didn't realize the domino effect that would follow. Suddenly, my siblings' friends who knew me from growing up might realize that if I'm a polygamist, then my brothers and sisters are, too. Several of my siblings who are still in high school became very angry with me for outing them by proxy.

Of all my relatives, my mother struggled the most with my decision. (She still blocks my posts on her Facebook page because she doesn't want to answer the intrusive questions that would follow. She isn't ready yet to be as open about her beliefs as I am.) When I told her about the show, she worried that I was putting my children in harm's way. She was especially concerned for them since my first marriage was destructive and unstable. I was just starting to figure out how to be a single mom. She felt that I was being irresponsible and not taking my children into consideration.

This was very difficult for me to hear. I understood her concerns, but I also knew that I was bringing my children into the most wonderful family I'd ever seen and giving them the best father imaginable. Although my mother will still be my mother privately, and supports me in every way she can, she wants nothing to do with the public side of my life. We love each other, but there is a distance between us that pains me.

My mother grew up LDS and converted to our faith when she was a young adult. Many of her relatives struggled with her conversion, so she has spent her life keeping her head down, feeling as if she had to apologize for her beliefs and try to not rub it in their faces. She hides her religion from the people around her and has to be careful about what she says and does. This has made me very sad.

However, after the show aired, many of my mother's relatives got a closer look at our world. They saw that our lifestyle was not scary or "out there." They were more able to understand my mother's decision to live the principle. Because of *Sister Wives*, my mother has been able to come into her own and feel more accepted by her own family. I hope that this change in her relatives' attitudes will allow my mother to live more openly and comfortably.

Like my mother, my father was opposed to my participation in *Sister Wives*. Although he is retired, he worked a city job his entire life, and had to hide his marriage to my mother. When I decided to be a part of the show, I think he worried about what would happen to me as well. But after he saw how people reacted to us after the show aired—approaching us on the street, wanting to talk to us, and writing encouraging letters—he began to relax and opened up to the show. In fact, he agreed to be filmed dancing with me at my wedding. This was a miracle for me. My father, who had never felt comfortable acknowledging me in public before, was willing to go on national television and announce that he is my dad. Later, my father agreed to be in an episode about our hunt for houses in Las Vegas. He was there while Meri, Kody, and I were looking for places for us to live. It meant so much to me that he consented to be filmed. Of all my family members, my father is the one who most recognizes and acknowledges all the positive changes the show has brought about.

Since filming was under way during Kody's and my long engagement, introducing Kody to my family meant bringing them face-to-face with the reality of my decision to be on television. When people started to recognize us, many family members shied away from me at public functions. They didn't want to be identified as polygamists.

Even when we weren't filming, many of my family members still wanted to keep their distance from me. My sister's gradu-

ation, an event I wouldn't have missed for the world, was especially trying. Kody and I tried to keep our heads down and
maintain a low profile, but we were recognized by many people
in the crowd. People were lining up to talk to us and get their pictures taken with us. I felt terrible, as my only intention had been
to support my sister on her special day, and now I was drawing
attention away from her.

Some of my brothers and sisters were simply embarrassed by
the people who wanted to take our picture. They hung back and
wouldn't associate with us at all. Thankfully, other members of
my family thought it was cool, like my sister who got so excited
when she saw how positively people were responding to Kody
and me. I think she was really surprised by how supportive complete strangers could be.

Several years before I married Kody, when I was at an absolute low point in my life, I made a life list of all the things I
wanted to accomplish. Since things were going so badly for me
at that time, I allowed myself to dream as big as possible. Here's
what was on my list: *change the world, meet Oprah, write a best-
seller, own a business.* I look back on that now and think, be careful what you wish for because you might get it—and then it may
be something you don't want. I can never underestimate the positive impact of *Sister Wives,* but there are days when I wake up
and say to myself, "I don't want to do this anymore. I want everything to go back to normal."

Being on a television show really altered my entry into the
family and into a plural marriage. Sadly, during the first season, many of our fans cast me as a home wrecker out to destroy
Meri, Janelle, and Christine's happy family. I try not to dwell on
the Internet commentary, but since I think it's important to interact with our fans, I can't entirely avoid it. There have been
so many negative comments about me that it's been difficult to

shrug them off. People believe I have an ulterior motive—that I want Kody to myself and not because I love the family or my sister wives. People believe I'm manipulative and conniving. I usually place last in the "Favorite Sister Wife" poll.

I know I should be stronger and not allow the opinions of our viewers to bother me. But so much of my marriage is tied up in the show, it's impossible not to be aware of the feedback and the audience reactions. I've had to be very open with Tim, our producer, and tell him that in certain areas he has to tread lightly so as not to give America's women another reason to hate me. If the audience dislikes me, then we've failed in our mission to convey the joys and the stability of our lifestyle. We want to dwell on the positives, not only on dramatic things that sully the picture, if only temporarily. Any woman living a plural life will tell you the struggles that we have shared about a new wife coming into a family are very normal and over time things get better.

It's ironic that the show itself was the catalyst for many of the troubles and struggles that we dealt with on camera. If not for the show, Kody and I would have married quickly and quietly with little fanfare.

The wedding became a storm cloud that hovered over us during the "couch sessions." Things that should have remained personal and private to Kody and me—things that could have been beautiful and special—were fodder for analysis. I had to deal with the world's opinion about the fact that Kody picked my dress. I had to deal with the world's thoughts about him kissing me during our engagement. Everybody on the couch—and in the audience—felt the need to participate in what seemed to be an endless commentary and judgment on my wedding, the reception, and the honeymoon. For me, at least, it cheapened and stripped away the beauty of something special. I felt that because of the show, nothing had been left for me. Huge portions of my life were turned into an open book available to public comment.

While the show certainly caused tensions to rise and tempers to flare concerning my marriage to Kody, it definitely paved the way for Kody and me to be open about our relationship. I don't know any plural wives who have had the freedom to publicly court and date and enjoy their husband's company in the same way that I have. This for me is one of the show's greatest blessings. The other blessing, of course, is creating a more tolerant world for our children.

Not long after the first season aired, Kody and I were at a restaurant near our house. It was obvious that we were on a romantic date—we were holding hands and being our usual affectionate selves. The waitress kept giving us the evil eye. I didn't understand her behavior. What had we done to upset her? Then Kody realized what was wrong. He'd been to the same restaurant with Meri a week earlier and been served by the same waitress. She obviously thought he was stepping out on his wife.

He wanted to let the misunderstanding slide. But I decided to speak up. "Excuse me," I said to the waitress. "I know that you think something strange is going on here. I wanted to clarify the situation. I am this man's wife. The woman you saw with him last week is also his wife. We are a plural family."

Her eyes widened, first in shock, then in realization. "Oh," she said, "you're that family from TV!" Immediately her demeanor changed from frosty to friendly.

It felt immensely liberating to be completely honest about our marriage. While I had my reservations about the show when Kody first mentioned it, I now know that it has been a remarkable step forward for our relationship.

More and more people recognize us these days, not just in our hometown, but all over the country. While I'm not comfortable with being called a "celebrity," I do love the outpouring of support we receive. I love it when I see that someone identifies with our family and is able to see that we all have something in common. Still, it's disconcerting when a person I've never met walks up to me on the street and starts talking as if she knows me, when she's only seen me on TV. Sometimes I want to say, "Don't judge me on the show alone." But I never say this, because people identify with our struggle and our decision to open our lives to the world. I don't want to alienate anyone.

Growing up polygamous has made me aware of all other repressed people in the world who are treated as second-class citizens on account of their beliefs, their choices, or their races and ethnicities. Living the way I do and being treated as I have been has made me extremely tolerant and open-minded. We all have the right to choose our partners in this life. Every adult should be able to choose whom to love and practice the faith of his or her choice. I hope that our story goes a long way toward making this possible in our community and for others who are persecuted. I feel confident that I will be able to check "change the world" off of my life list.

One of the other things on that list that I have been able to check off is "meet Oprah." Oprah has always been one of my heroes, a person I respect in all ways. When I put this goal on my list, I never in my wildest dreams imagined it would come true. So I was astonished when our publicist booked us on *Oprah* to promote the show.

Before we went to Chicago for the taping, I rehearsed in my mind what I would say to Oprah. When things were at their worst in my life—during the end of my first marriage and divorce—I would watch *Oprah* every afternoon with tears running down my face. "This woman is so wonderful," I'd say aloud, even if there was no one in the room. I wanted to tell her this. I wanted to let her know how much she had meant to me during my hard times. She was the bright spot in my day. *Oprah* was my favorite escape.

When we arrived at the set for the *Oprah* show, it looked nothing like it did on TV—pristine and graceful, awash in soft colors and low lights. Instead it was rickety. The furniture looked temporary. It was cold. It felt more like a warehouse than a studio. Onstage, with my microphone on, I felt distant from the audience and the whole *Oprah* experience.

When you watch *Oprah* on TV, it is a magical experience. The environment is warm and friendly. It's a place for dreams and aspirations. But sitting there in that cold soundstage, I realized that *Oprah* is just a television show. Like all other television programs, it creates fantasies for the at-home viewers. It's part make-believe. It invites them into a world that doesn't entirely exist. I realized that the magic I had watched on TV wasn't real.

It was interesting to watch Oprah deal with her team of producers and camerapeople. We watched her take care of mundane details that go into producing her show every day. Without the high gloss of the television camera, Oprah could have been any other businesswoman.

When the show assistants sat me down beside her, I took my chance. I leaned over to her and told her she was wonderful and an inspiration to me. She was so humble and sweet. I realized then that Oprah was just a woman like me. She probably dealt with the same kind of scrutiny and pressure the camera and an audience can put on you as I did, just in a bigger way. I realized that I had made her into some sort of demi-god when she probably had just been doing what she felt like God had called her to do. It really grounded me and made me realize that, TV or not, we are all just people trying to get through the day.

Being on *Sister Wives* has taught me so much about myself

and others. I have realized that while *Sister Wives* tells our story, the real magic is in our own home. No matter how many televised interviews I do, how many famous people I meet, how many seasons our own show runs, there is one constant in my life. What matters to me when the dust settles and the lights are turned off is what mattered before all of this started: my family, my faith, my love, and my responsibility to myself and others.

EPILOGUE

Kody

When we decided to tell our story, I figured that the benefits would outweigh the risks. I wanted to make the world a better place, not just for my family but for polygamists worldwide. I wanted to show the public how wonderfully stable, loving, and caring my family is. I thought we might pave the way for a safer and more tolerant future for our community.

Nevertheless, it wasn't a decision I made without careful consideration, prayer, and consultation with all my wives. I wanted to proceed with caution. I had thought that in deciding to do a reality show, I would help to bring other plural families out into the open so they could benefit from society as all other citizens do. While I feel terrible if *Sister Wives* has driven any fundamentalist Mormons back into hiding, I do feel, for my family at least, that the benefits far outweigh the costs. The fact that my family can live openly is one of the greatest miracles I have witnessed in my lifetime, a miracle that I had never even dreamed was possible until recently. I love that all my wives are accepted as my spouses. This has given us a great boost of confidence as well as made us stronger as a family.

Our move to Las Vegas changed my life irrevocably. I felt an overwhelming peace and tranquillity with our arrival. I felt as if we had moved to a world of opportunity. To put it simply, I felt safe. But although I felt a new spiritual peace, we had sacrificed so much from our lives in Utah—the transition was for the best, but it was still difficult. Janelle and I had left thriving careers. We had all moved away from the fellowship of our church and our dearest friends. We left behind the most wonderful home our family had ever lived in, and one of the safest communities in the country. Our children had done the same, without sharing their parents' understanding about why. I was shell-shocked from the stress of our lives during the sixty days before the move. During the move, I felt deeply bitter about the whole experience of becoming a public polygamist. Frankly, my own tolerance and open-mindedness meant that I was naive about how living publicly would effect us as a family.

Why did we leave? I am a husband and a father first, and as a parent, my first responsibility is to keep the family safe. Our simple world in the sleepy town of Lehi, Utah, became very volatile in the fall of 2010 due to the investigation and the stresses of our family becoming public polygamists. We no longer felt that our family was safe. By the beginning of December, all five parents agreed that our family would be better off in Las Vegas. By Christmastime, we had told the older children.

They were very upset by the news. At first, Mariah was so opposed to leaving her home and her friends that she flat out refused to move. Finally, just three days before our move, we told the younger children. Some were excited, some were shattered. Paedon stayed in his bed for two days. It wasn't pretty, but we figured the collateral damage of our children's emotions was a small thing compared to some of the trouble and attitudes we were experiencing as a family in Utah. Our children did not agree that moving was the right thing to do. They did understand, however, that the family needed to do whatever was necessary to stay together. I don't believe they fully understood the need to move away until we had been in Vegas for several months.

We rented a temporary vacation home in Las Vegas for thirty days in order to stage an aggressive search for new homes from this shared location. We acquired the rental and made the agreement only days before we left Lehi. We were literally living day to day. Life in the vacation home was a bit of a struggle. Everybody had become used to his or her own space and autonomy in Lehi. Now I had four wives sharing one kitchen and only four bedrooms. There were no specific rooms for the children. So we placed older girls in the family room, older boys in the living room, and the younger children in the bedrooms with their own mothers. Our first priority was getting the kids in school. We felt right about a particular high school, so we needed first to find a home in that specific school area. The school district does not allow transient enrollment into the school, so we needed to get a permanent address from which to enroll the children. We decided for the sake of Robyn's children, who weren't as used to living in such a big family, and who had already moved so often in the previous two years, that we should find her a home first. We moved her just in time for the teens to start high school in January.

Back in Lehi, I had coined our move "the Vegas Vacation" in order to keep our attitudes positive about the whole move experience. We had no idea how much work was cut out for us. We moved four complete households in a matter of four calendar weeks. That way we were out of the vacation home as contracted and living in the school area we wanted. This move was exhausting. I felt as if we were constantly working to finish the production of the TV show for the season, while documenting the whole move experience for the following season. We were working our tails off and still had the pressure to get jobs and a real life going again.

In spite of the wonderful sunshine and beautiful sunsets in Las Vegas, everybody was a bit off. The elementary school children—Dayton, Gabriel, Gwendlyn, Aurora, Ysabel, Breanna, and Savanah—were adjusting very well to school. However, the tight integration of our family culture seemed to be eroding in significant ways. Janelle and Christine had been running their households almost as if they were a single unit, and now they lived a half mile apart. Gabriel and Gwendlyn, who have birthdays four days apart and have grown up almost as twins, are no longer living in connected homes. The structure and help with school that Christine had given Janelle's children was no longer available. Our high school kids were welcomed warmly by their peers, but their hearts were still connected to Utah. Now our family was separated. One friend of ours suggested that we were experiencing something very similar to a divorce. We no longer lived together, and the adjustment was damaging our well-being.

As time went by while living in Las Vegas, other problems arose. Hunter, for whatever reason, maybe out of love and loyalty to his football team in Lehi (state runners-up two years in row!) refused to play football. He actually refused even to make friends. He seemed to sink deeper and deeper into depression as the summer came closer. Nobody knew what to do for him. His counselor at school told us not to worry until it had persisted for six months. At least his grades remained good.

All these things shook our family to the foundation. I had only married Robyn a year ago, and we were still getting used to being a family. Now we had to change everything again, and work together as adults on more than just our marriages and managing family matters. The move had all of us reevaluating our relationships and our individual identities. We had to clean house, emotionally speaking. We needed to detox our relationships and some of our deepest issues. The family needed to get well, both the children and the parents.

When I reflect on the personal growth and development of our family over the years, I am pleased and overwhelmed. Getting to where we are now from where we had been has been a long process. I reflect back on my life and see how much we have grown from those immature places of years gone by and wonder, Will I be as pleased with our emotional growth over the next ten years? Will I look back at this past year and think, boy, was I immature? During the sixteen years before Robyn came into the family, Meri, Janelle, Christine, and I had a lot of growing to do. In the last five years, before Robyn entered the family, we really had found a very comfortable groove. We were stable and generally happy. The children were well adjusted and very happy. Something was missing though. Our individual marriages and the sister wife relationships were far from ideal.

In years past, when Meri, Janelle, Christine, and I used to have family meetings about money concerns, kids' problems at school, or any of the other things married couples deal with, it was hard not to become defensive, and I would often feel antagonistic. I tried to understand all the charged emotions coming at me from three different directions. My patience would grow short and we would not communicate as well as an enlightened family should. This was all in our most recent years. We were even worse back when we were all new at it and the oldest children were toddlers. I knew that in our acceptance of the principle of plural marriage, we were being challenged to be kinder, more patient, and more loving in our mundane day-to-day life. We didn't always rise to the occasion. We needed improvement in our relationships, and we didn't even know it

Robyn and I had been courting for about two months when we got engaged. She had been received by Meri, Janelle, and

Christine with open hearts and open arms. Within a month of our engagement, however, everybody started to struggle with the emotional adjustments of the courtship. Robyn quickly realized that we had been avoiding many of our problems. In my pride, I had rejected the idea of any form of marriage counseling. We did not know how to validate each other in our feelings. We were hiding our problems in career pursuits and other outward efforts. In our marriages, and the sister wife relationships, we had started to settle for less than our best. We became complacent with mediocre lives, relationships, and marriages. There was nothing wrong with that if we didn't mind living a mundane life. However, plural marriage is only lived well when those involved seek to strengthen and better their relationships. Some of us had become aggressive, some of us had buried our feelings, and we weren't emotionally healthy enough to have another wife come into the family. I put off the wedding until the following spring because we didn't have the financial means to support Robyn and her family—but we actually needed that time to heal our relationships so that Robyn could enter a family that was ready for another wife.

Families living plural marriage have to expect emotional and spiritual growth. Our move to Nevada brought on new problems we never expected. We started working together to find and build businesses. Many married people love each other very much, but enjoy time apart while they immerse themselves in a career. Most people will tell you that it is a struggle to work in business with their spouse. Many tell me they could *never* work in business with their husband or wife. Now I am working every day, and in every way, with all four of my wives. This experience has caused us some significant new challenges. My wives are all very independent, free-thinking women. They each have a mind of their own, and frequently like to give me a piece of it. Getting consensus is somewhat like pulling teeth. Some days when we first moved to the four homes, I wanted to just walk away. I actually got tired of working with them all the time. There were many days when I thought we wouldn't be able to pull it off. I just kept telling myself that it was necessary. If I want to be with them for all of this life and beyond, I had sure better be able to work with them in a business.

Part of our struggle was actually agreeing on a business that worked for the whole family. Our insecurities were brought to the surface again and again, trying to figure out what business suited everyone. Magic happened when all my wives started training with a fitness coach. He and I had become friends and were obsessed with the idea of opening a fitness center together. My wives loved this idea. As we formulated a plan, we were approached by a company that asked our family to partner with them on Operation Detox, a business and humanitarian project focusing on nutrition and addiction recovery. Both these endeavors gave the family new direction and purpose. Our relationships are thriving with the new energy of having a cause to unite the family with something we *all* felt passionate about. This new direction even engaged the kids.

As our family united on the wellness and fitness center projects, other things began to fall into place. The older children began to show positive signs of adjusting. Aspyn said that she had always loved living in Las Vegas, and Mykelti agreed with her. Madison began to enjoy her social life, not needing her Utah friends so desperately. Hunter started playing on the high school football team and in spite of joining late, became the defensive standout on his freshman team. Logan is on the wrestling team and has already qualified for the varsity position. Mariah lettered in tennis and has made some dear friends. Gabriel and Gwendlyn, our separated "twins," have learned to express their need to spend time together and we always facilitate it. All these things have been punctuated by the comfortable adjustment of Paedon,

Dayton, and Garrison becoming video game buddies and enjoying middle school together. Last of all, the "pixies," as I call all the little girls, enjoy frequent sleepovers, playing dolls and dress-up at each other's homes. The "Vegas Vacation" became a reality for me this past summer as the kids began to relax into their new lives while we spent time as a whole family at Janelle's pool.

My family is my life. I love being in a peaceful and happy environment with them. I draw strength from them daily. I love the energy and unity that we exude as a group. After all, ours is the ultimate love story, sweet, layered, textured, passionate, and tender. It is complicated, as all marriages are. To know true love you need to understand the struggles that come with it. Within these struggles, we have found that our true love can endure with commitment. To be the best person you can be, the best father, the best husband, the best citizen of this earth, you have to confront your weaknesses and overcome obstacles the world puts in your path. As part of my life path, I have had to learn to love without conditions. I have needed to learn how to validate emotions and feelings that I do not understand. I have had to be empathetic and patient. I have had to grow in this capacity to be more loving to my wives, so that their lives are also rich and fulfilled. This is what makes plural marriage so sacred to me— this calling to transcend my limitations, to learn from others on a daily basis, to learn to accept. True love comes not from resting on your laurels but from hard work, devotion, dedication, and commitment.

I'm sure that there are millions of people in the world who misinterpret what I do as hedonistic and selfish. My response is: Every day I work my tail off for this family. Every day I manage four separate marriages, four entirely different relationships, four distinct personalities. I'm not doing this for fun and games. I'm doing it because it is my calling. I'm doing it because of my faith. I do it for *love*! Before anyone thinks that polygamy is easy or uncomplicated, I urge them to consider how much work a single marriage takes—and then multiply that times four.

No one ever said that following your convictions was easy. However, I completely believe that all the work pays off. I have been blessed with so many things—beautiful wives, incredible children, and the chance to tell my story to the world. With all this love, who could ask for more?

ACKNOWLEDGMENTS

We are grateful for the efforts of Tim Gibbons and Christopher Poole of Puddle Monkey Productions and all our friends at Figure 8 Films and TLC. They have protected our story and made it possible for us to tell the truth about our lives.

We are grateful to Principle Voices for their pioneering work in opening the Fundamentalist Mormon communities.

We appreciate those friends who have shown us love and support as we have done what we felt was right.

Thanks to our parents and families for their support, and for being instrumental in shaping us into the people we are today.

Above all, we give thanks to God for giving our lives direction and blessing us so abundantly.